Observing Dimensions of Learning in Classrooms and Schools

John L. Brown

ASCD

Association for Supervision and Curriculum Development
Alexandria, Virginia

ASCD

Association for Supervision and Curriculum Development
1250 N. Pitt Street • Alexandria, Virginia 22314
Telephone: (703) 549-9110 • Fax: (703) 299-8631

Gene R. Carter, *Executive Director*
Michelle Terry, *Assistant Executive Director, Program Development*
Ronald S. Brandt, *Assistant Executive Director*
Nancy Modrak, *Managing Editor, ASCD Books*
Julie Houtz, *Sr. Associate Editor*

Carolyn Cottom, *Copy Editor*
Gary Bloom, *Manager, Design and Production* Services
Tracey Smith, *Print Production Coordinator*
Valerie Sprague, *Desktop Publisher*

Printed in the United States of America.

From the Editors: We welcome readers' comments on ASCD books and other publications. If you would like to give us your opinion of this book or suggest topics for future books, please write to ASCD, Managing Editor of Books, 1250 N. Pitt St., Alexandria, VA 22314.

ASCD Stock No.: 195209 $13.95   S11/95

Library of Congress Cataloging-in-Publication Data
Brown, John L., 1947-
  Observing dimensions of learning in classrooms and schools / John
L. Brown.
    p. cm.
  Includes bibliographical references and index.
  ISBN 0-87120-255-7 (pbk.)
  1. Thought and thinking—Study and teaching. 2. Observation
(Educational method) 3. Cognitive learning I. Association for
Supervision and Curriculum Development. II. Title.
LB1590.3.B757 1995
370.15'2—dc20   95-32520
                                                 CIP

99   98   97   96   10   9   8   7   6   5   4   3   2   1

OBSERVING DIMENSIONS OF LEARNING IN CLASSROOMS AND SCHOOLS

Foreword   *Robert J. Marzano*   v

1   Introduction   1

2   Observing the Dimensions of the Learning Organization   6

3   Observation in Transition   22

4   Beginning with the End in Mind: Observing Dimension 5   30

5   Reinforcing Authenticity in the Classroom: Observing
    Dimension 4   46

6   Supporting Students' Mastery of a Core Curriculum:
    Observing Dimension 2   61

7   Internalizing the Language of Thinking: Observing
    Dimension 3   76

8   Addressing and Enhancing the Affective Domain:
    Observing Dimension 1   86

9   Professional Development and Observing Dimensions of
    Learning   99

10 One School System's Story   113

Appendix A: Integrating Dimensions of Learning
    into the Formal Teacher Observation Process   125

References and Resources   139

About the Author   142

Foreword

When a group of some 90 educators first convened in 1989 to begin field-testing what was then a skeletal framework called Dimensions of Learning, I had hopes that educators outside of this small cadre would one day share our enthusiasm for this model of organizing teaching and learning. Today, more than 50,000 educators have participated in Dimensions of Learning training and, from the reports my colleagues and I have received, many really are finding the model most useful in their work.

One of the characteristics the original development group consciously tried to build into the framework was flexibility. Specifically, we hoped the model could be adapted to uses beyond the classroom by a wide variety of educational practitioners. This exciting book by John Brown does just that. It applies the foundational elements of the Dimensions of Learning model to the work of school administrators, integrating those elements with the concepts and practices considered the cornerstones of administrative practice. In fact, *Observing Dimensions of Learning in Classrooms and Schools* can be used by at least four audiences: building-level administrators working with teachers who are using the Dimensions of Learning (DoL) model, central office administrators in districts that are using the model as a catalyst for organizational change, individuals training others to use the model, and teachers using the model in their classrooms.

The most obvious audience for this book is building-level administrators working with teachers who are trying to use the DoL strategies in their classrooms. For this group, Brown's book offers practical methods for integrating Dimensions of Learning with such tested administrative tools as clinical supervision and cognitive coaching. Additionally, it provides building administrators with detailed observation instruments for each of the five dimensions of learning and a highly useful trouble-shooting guide that recommends specific solutions to specific problems.

For central office administrators, the book offers explicit guidelines for using the framework as a tool for restructuring policies regarding curriculum, instruction, and assessment. Brown quite masterfully uses the principles of organizational change articulated by noted experts such as Stephen Covey and Peter Senge to support these guidelines. Woven throughout the many practical illustrations and tools provided by Brown is the message that districts must make a commitment to "transform" themselves rather than just "tinker" with details if the results are to be worth the effort.

For those interested in training others to use the Dimensions of Learning model, this book offers explicit guidance on how to establish a sound training environment, how to sequence and pace training for maximum effect, and how to determine the effectiveness of training. Brown also provides detailed descriptions of how to use specific episodes from ASCD's *Video Library of Teaching Episodes* as aids in training. Each episode cited by Brown is not only keyed to specific dimensions, but to specific techniques within a given dimension.

For teachers, *Observing Dimensions of Learning in Classrooms and Schools* provides a firm grounding in how to overcome the complexity of the Dimensions of Learning model and shape it into a tool that meets their specific needs. Teachers will especially appreciate the strategies and observational instruments for assessing students' progress in each of the five dimensions.

Brown couches his discussion of Dimensions of Learning in the context of Senge's concept of the "learning organization"—that is, an organization "where people are continually learning how to learn together." Thus, a district, school, or teacher that follows Brown's recommendations not only implements Dimensions of Learning, but also develops the ability to initiate and sustain a plethora of future innovations. We can see this process at work in Brown's detailed case study illustrating how educators in his own school district, the Prince George's County Public Schools in Maryland, are using the Dimensions of Learning model to guide their change process.

I have admired John Brown's intellect, effort, and integrity from the day I met him. As the spokesperson for the Dimensions of Learning author team, I express my sincere gratitude for his involvement with Dimensions of Learning and, most especially, for this fine book. Whether or not you're familiar with Dimensions of Learning, I think you'll come away from this book eager to try out some of John Brown's ideas in your own classroom, school, or district.

—ROBERT J. MARZANO
Mid-continent Regional Educational Laboratory
Aurora, Colorado, July 1995

1

Introduction

This book represents a journey that began in 1992 with the publication of the *Dimensions of Learning Teacher's Manual* (Marzano, Pickering, Arredondo, Blackburn, Brandt, and Moffett 1992a). At that time, my school system, the Prince George's County Public Schools, implemented the Dimensions of Learning program as part of a systemwide adoption by the state of Maryland. Those of us in the initial training group were struck by how right the program felt: It appeared to be a long-overdue answer to our search for a viable way to improve the thinking skills of the students in our school system, currently the 17th largest in the United States.

At the same time, we were aware that Dimensions of Learning would require each of us to "own" the program if we were to assist others in adopting it. As the old adage reminds us, the longest journey begins with the first step, but none of us had any idea how powerful, profound, and complex the Dimensions of Learning adoption and implementation journey ultimately would become for all of us.

As seems to be true with any successful program innovation, those of us who were early adopters struggled to internalize the program and its rich variety of strategies, interventions, and design elements. At times overwhelmed by the seeming complexity of the program, we eventually became a community of learners, working together to operationalize its language, define what specific program components meant to us and our school system, and develop a meaningful strategic plan for training the 6,500 educators who constitute our professional staff.

After numerous overview sessions and two-day trainings for teachers, administrators, and curriculum specialists, the members of the original training group became aware that building a support structure for follow-up and program implementation was absolutely critical. If program adoption were to occur at a systemic level, we had to make structural changes in all parts of our system that were consistent with the principles and design features of the Dimensions of Learning model.

Perhaps most significantly, we realized that if the model were to succeed in our system, we had to arrive at some form of agreement about what evidence would be present if the program were fully operational. What, in effect, could we *observe* if the school system were successfully "dimensionized"? How would a school site function and what organizational behaviors would we observe if Dimensions of Learning were operational there? Finally, what would we observe in the way of transformed behaviors among our supervisory and administrative staff, our teachers, and, most importantly, our students as they moved through the K–12 program? Out of these dialogues and shared inquiry the seeds for this book were sown.

The ideas, suggestions, and observation instruments that make up this publication represent a synthesis of the insights, practices, and conclusions associated with the Dimensions of Learning implementation process within my particular school system. At the same time, I believe that what we have learned can be of great value to other systems embarking on the Dimensions of Learning pathway. I am particularly indebted to Ron Brandt, Bob Marzano, Debra Pickering, and Cerylle Moffett for their encouragement during the writing of this book. Through their insights and support I have been able to transcend what was, on occasion, slightly myopic thinking about the nature of the observation process as it related to Dimensions of Learning.

As a result of my dialogues with these members of the original author team, the book now encompasses a much richer and comprehensive view of the process of observing for Dimensions of Learning. Rather than restricting the concept of observation to the clinical supervision of teachers in the classroom, I have broadened my focus to include preliminary answers to the following observation questions:

- What are the observable characteristics and behaviors of a learning organization[1] that is successfully implementing the Dimensions of Learning program?

- What behaviors and processes should we be able to observe in a school system moving toward successful implementation; that is, integrating Dimensions of Learning in a way that promotes systemwide changes in curriculum, instruction, assessment, and student achievement?

- What specific practices should be evident in a district's teacher observation process? How can a school system's repertoire of teacher observation practices be enhanced to ensure consistency with the philosophy, principles, and strategies of Dimensions of Learning?

- How can teacher observation be transformed into a process of collaboration and mutual learning? How can partnership approaches such as cognitive coaching, peer coaching, and action research complement existing clinical supervision practices?

[1]As defined by Senge (1990), a learning organization is one that is able to renew itself because there is a collective commitment to eliminating roadblocks to professional growth, product development, or internal communications due to outmoded barriers or structures.

- For each of the five dimensions of learning, what observable evidence should be present at a school site if a particular dimension has been successfully implemented?
- Are there models or examples that an observer can use to improve his or her ability to provide meaningful oral and written feedback to a teacher being observed for the use of a particular dimension of learning in his or her classroom?

The purpose of this book is to explore the process of observing for Dimensions of Learning (DoL) in as comprehensive and expansive a way as possible. Its central goal is to provide ideas and strategies for observers involved in all aspects of implementation. A school staff just beginning to explore the program, for example, can use these materials to assess the extent to which DoL techniques and practices are already in operation at the school. Individuals or complete staffs engaged in ongoing DoL training can use many of the resources presented here to monitor their progress during the adoption process. Central office administrators and curriculum supervisors can make use of key elements of the book to assess their own progress in facilitating meaningful changes in curriculum, instruction, and assessment. Perhaps most significantly, the materials presented here offer numerous ways for educators to evaluate their role in transforming classrooms into centers of learning.

Toward these ends, *Observing Dimensions of Learning in Classrooms and Schools* has been organized so that the individual practitioner or study group can access its resources from a variety of entry points. Chapter 2, for example, is titled "Observing the Dimensions of the Learning Organization." Using Peter Senge's (1990) concept of "metanoia" (the process of expressing a group's commitment to improving self-knowledge and self-awareness within a learning organization), this chapter begins with an overview of the key structural elements and group processes that one should observe in a school system successfully adopting the Dimensions of Learning model. The material includes descriptions of proposed changes in curriculum and assessment at a systemic level. The chapter also presents self-assessment questionnaires that individuals and full staffs can use to determine where they perceive themselves to be along an adoption continuum. Included are three questionnaires based on the major design principles and interventions associated with each of the five dimensions of learning.

Chapter 3, "Observation in Transition," explores the rich variety of options in the field of teacher observation today. Increasingly, research studies confirm the enormous value of practitioner-based collaboration as a complement to traditional clinical supervision practices. Chapter 3 encourages teachers to use the materials related to cognitive and peer coaching practices to enhance their performance. The chapter also encourages instructors and other school-based staff members to use action research projects in their classrooms and school sites to complement the Dimensions of Learning implementation process. Action research can become a vehicle for effective problem solving and decision making, enriching the research and knowledge base available to school and system staff in the process.

Chapters 4 through 8 present specific profiles of the five dimensions of learning as an extension of the issues and principles presented more globally in the previous chapters. In each of chapters 4 through 8, the reader is given suggestions for collecting evidence to confirm that a particular dimension of learning has become operational at a system, school, or classroom level. Wherever possible, these chapters avoid a checklist approach in favor of a series of program evaluation questions, guiding principles, and teacher observation suggestions that can be used to monitor DoL implementation in a specific site or classroom.

These chapters have been organized to reinforce the nonlinear nature of the Dimensions of Learning model. Chapter 4, for example, titled "Beginning With the End in Mind," focuses on observing Dimension 5, Productive Habits of Mind. After exploring the role of cognitive habits in an effective learning organization, the next chapter backward-maps from Dimension 5 to Dimension 4, Meaningful-Use Tasks, discussing how authentic independent learning projects can provide a perfect context for demonstrating productive habits of mind.

The book next explores how Dimension 2, Acquiring and Integrating Knowledge, and Dimension 3, Extending and Refining Knowledge, can be used to prepare students for success in completing meaningful-use tasks and applying productive mental habits. It then addresses the critically important element of how students' affective needs can be met through successful implementation of Dimension 1, Developing Positive Attitudes and Perceptions About Learning.

All of these chapters emphasize the observation phenomena associated with each of the dimensions, including perspectives on ways that clinical supervisors, cognitive coaches, peer coaches, and action research teams can investigate the dimensions and use the observation process to improve teacher and student performance. Each chapter concludes with a detailed set of examples of observation feedback. These are suggestions for how post-observation conferences and written feedback can be structured when observing for each of the five dimensions of learning. It is hoped that the examples will prove useful to DoL study teams engaged in adopting and implementing the model.

As we have discovered in my own school system, every school, every staff, and every individual educator will construct an understanding of DoL in a slightly different way. Just as every school site has its own unique climate and organizational culture, every system, site, or classroom will manifest DoL implementation in a way consistent with the norms, mores, and standards of that setting and organizational context. Therefore, the materials in this book should be viewed as road maps or "trip-tiks," aids to support a collaborative journey of discovery, exploration, and program implementation, rather than as fixed lists of "must-do's" and "must-haves."

The final chapters of *Observing Dimensions of Learning in Classrooms and Schools* attempt to make the preceding materials even more concrete and practical by describing examples of how they have been used in actual practice. Chapter 9, "Professional Development and Observing Dimensions of Learning," provides a brief overview of how the materials in this book can be used along with resources such as the videotape programs *The Video Library of Teaching Episodes* (ASCD 1988) and *The Teaching Strategies Library* (ASCD 1987/1989) to develop and implement successful professional development experiences related to observing for Dimensions of Learning. When combined with videotaped teaching episodes of teachers at work in their own classrooms, these materials offer staff developers, administrators, and curriculum specialists a set of tools for making DoL concrete and meaningful in their learning organizations.

Finally, Chapter 10, "One School System's Story," profiles how the Prince George's County Public Schools in Maryland have integrated Dimensions of Learning into all facets of the school improvement planning process, including training for new teachers and a formal observation process for all educators in the system. Preliminary results of our system's DoL implementation process are described as well.

I am continually struck by the metaphor of the Dimensions of Learning implementation process as a journey of self-discovery and shared inquiry. The observation process can become a vehicle for sharing insights and suggestions about how to make sure that this journey is a successful and productive one. As suggested in many great works of world literature and philosophy, the value of the journey is in its taking, not just in where it leads us. Through the process of shared exploration, we discover more completely who we are as educators and as human beings. In turn, we enhance our students' ability to grow as lifelong learners. As the poet T. S. Eliot writes in *Four Quartets*:

> We shall not cease from exploration
> And the end of all our exploring
> Will be to arrive where we started
> And know the place for the first time.

2

Observing the Dimensions of the Learning Organization

Dimensions of Learning is a program designed to improve students' thinking skills that provides a comprehensive basis for instructional planning and curriculum design. It is also a powerful model for staff development related to thinking skills improvement. Based on the best of current research in learning theory and cognitive psychology, Dimensions of Learning is the product of a collaboration between the Association for Supervision and Curriculum Development and a team of authors headed by Robert J. Marzano of the Mid-continent Regional Educational Laboratory. School systems and school sites in many countries, including the United States, have adopted the program because they recognize its unique contribution to curricular and instructional reform and school-based instructional decision making.

Using feedback from extensive field testing by nearly 90 educators, Marzano and his co-authors developed a practical way to transform traditional schooling into a learning-centered approach that meets these five criteria:

1. Instruction should reflect the best of what we know about how learning occurs.

- New learning is shaped by the learner's *prior knowledge*. Good instruction dignifies and draws upon that knowledge.

- Much learning occurs through *social interaction*. Effective instruction should acknowledge the social and cultural nature of the learning process.

- Learning is closely *tied to particular situations*. The "situated" nature of the process suggests that transfer of a body of information or a skill does not occur easily or automatically. Teachers must plan for transfer in every lesson and unit.

- Successful learning involves students' *use of numerous strategies, each of which can be taught and reinforced*. Ideally, students are helped to incorporate these strategies into a personal repertoire of learning skills that can become a foundation for lifelong learning.

- Wherever possible, learning events should be *experience-based* and related to the world beyond the classroom.

2. Learning is an interactive process involving five forms or dimensions of thinking.

- Dimension 1: Positive attitudes and perceptions about learning.
- Dimension 2: Thinking used to acquire and integrate knowledge.
- Dimension 3: Thinking used to extend and refine knowledge.
- Dimension 4: Thinking involved in using knowledge meaningfully.
- Dimension 5: Productive habits of mind.

3. The K–12 curricula should include explicit teaching of attitudes, perceptions, and mental habits that facilitate learning.

4. Comprehensive approaches to instruction should include both teacher-directed and student-directed activity.

5. Assessment should focus on students' reasoning and use of knowledge rather than on their recall of information.

How can schools and school systems ensure that these principles become an integral part of all facets of their educational program? How can educational institutions beginning to implement Dimensions of Learning transform themselves into successful learning organizations? Working together to adopt and implement Dimensions of Learning is a powerful opportunity to transform both staff and student behavior relative to critical, creative, and self-regulated thinking. No process of meaningful systemic reform, however, is a simple one. In his ground-breaking book *The Fifth Discipline*, Senge (1990) compares the experience to the ways in which people describe being part of a highly effective team:

> People talk about being part of something larger than themselves, of being connected, of being generative. It becomes quite clear that, for many, their experiences as part of truly great teams stand out as singular periods of life lived to the fullest. Some spend the rest of their lives looking for ways to recapture that spirit (p. 13).

For Senge, transforming an organization through the adoption of a change element like Dimensions of Learning requires a collective commitment to the process of "metanoia"—a collective shift of mind. Schools and school systems seeking this institutional shift need to articulate and internalize the goals of successful Dimensions of Learning implementation at an individual, group, and system level. As Senge points out, a learning organization encourages all of its members to practice individually and collectively the essence of real learning, which, he suggests,

. . . gets to the heart of what it means to be human. Through learning we re-create ourselves. Through learning we re-perceive the world and our relationship to it. Through learning we extend our capacity to create, to be part of the generative process of life (p. 14).

The authors of Dimensions of Learning identify a four-level process of implementation. At Level 1, an organization collaborates on helping teachers and district leaders assess the degree to which they are already addressing each of the dimensions in their instructional and staff development program. This initial phase of adoption is critical in reinforcing the collective awareness that Dimensions of Learning is intended as a synthesis of the best practices available—those that are designed to sustain constructivist, learner-centered classrooms. It is imperative that staff not view it as just one more program to implement, but as a confirmation of what many teachers are already doing effectively to facilitate student learning. This first level of adoption becomes, in effect, a process of language acquisition, with the organization exploring the alignment between Dimensions of Learning and existing curriculum and instructional design and practice.

Level 2 implementation focuses on increasing teachers' repertoire of instructional strategies. Traditional staff development sessions that present overviews of Dimensions of Learning are almost inevitable at this point, but a true learning organization will ensure that such sessions are complemented by a wide variety of professional development enhancements. Training school-based teams that include at least one administrator, for example, will ensure that the program is not something that is "done to" teachers, but becomes, instead, a vehicle for exploring the entire instructional process at a school site. Parallel sessions might also be provided for administrators and curriculum specialists who will be working closely with teachers to implement the techniques and strategies presented in training sessions.

Perhaps most significantly, schools and school systems at Level 2 implementation can begin to explore ways of transforming significant linkage documents (e.g., lesson plan formats, Scope and Sequence frameworks, program overviews) to reflect the language of Dimensions of Learning. The greater the evidence of DoL principles and techniques in all aspects of the instructional process, the greater the likelihood that DoL will have a significant impact on the long-range operations of the learning organization.

When a school or school system has moved to Level 3 implementation, experienced teachers and instructional supervisors and specialists will participate in guided practice in using Dimensions of Learning unit planning guides to design new units of instruction. As many DoL adopters have discovered in the process of designing these units and the daily lesson plans that follow, the practitioner begins to internalize and "own" the model.

Unlike the sometimes clean and controlled process of large-group training sessions, unit planning sessions and clinics can become messy and sometimes frustrating, but they are almost always deeply engaging. Through unit planning, teachers and instructional specialists begin to discover the interconnections among the five dimensions of learning. In the process, practitioners construct meaning about the model at a deep and practical level, taking into consideration the unique needs of their students and the specific performance outcomes they are responsible for helping those students to master. This level of implementation is an important time for the learning organization to reexamine its entire curriculum design and development process, including the format it uses to present written curriculum.

Finally, Level 4 implementation, as described by the Dimensions of Learning author team, requires a collective commitment to reinventing the entire school system as a learning organization. During this phase, the DoL framework becomes "a vehicle for fundamental systemwide change in curriculum, instruction, and assessment in response to a school or district's own initiatives or to external mandates for school reform" (Marzano, Pickering, Arredondo, Blackburn, Brandt, and Moffett 1992b, pp. 28-29). At a systemwide level, a Dimensions of Learning organization is committed to the following long-term goals:

- To build an interdisciplinary curriculum that supports the integration of diverse, increasingly complex thinking and content knowledge.

- To increase teachers' skill in using instructional strategies that enhance students' use of all five dimensions of learning.

- To develop authentic forms of assessment that provide more valuable and authentic information about students and programs, engage students in performance-based tasks, and drive such desired changes as the implementation of performance-based instruction.

Becoming a Level 4 Dimensions of Learning organization requires a deep-seated, collective vision for educational reform. What specifically should be observable when this vision begins to manifest? The authors of the program emphasize that all members of the school site or school system must share this collective vision and be engaged together in ongoing transformation of three areas:

- *Their curriculum* (moving from a program that emphasizes content-specific knowledge and skills to one that balances content knowledge, complex thinking processes, strategies for developing positive habits of mind, and interdisciplinary tasks that require students to apply knowledge and skills in meaningful ways);

- *Their instruction* (moving from a teacher-centered approach to a learner-centered, outcome-based approach that involves students in acquiring and integrating knowledge, monitoring their own learning, and applying knowledge and skills in complex ways); and
- *Their approach to assessment and program evaluation* (moving from an approach emphasizing objective, recall-based, paper-and-pencil tests to one emphasizing outcomes and authentic assessments of student performance in important curriculum content areas).

For educators to realize this vision, they must modify traditional bureaucratic structures that reinforce the status quo to make certain that all parts of an organization practice metanoia, a process that involves self-reflection, joint inquiry, and mutual support to encourage both personal and organizational mastery. A Dimensions of Learning organization should continually reflect its commitment to the growth of its people:

> People with high levels of personal mastery are more committed. They take more initiative. They have a broader and deeper sense of responsibility in their work. They learn faster. For all these reasons, a great many organizations espouse a commitment to fostering personal growth among their employees because they believe it will make the organization stronger (Senge 1990, p. 143).

In working to implement a learning organization consistent with the principles and values of Dimensions of Learning, staffs must engage in an ongoing process of vision setting, mental modeling, and strategic planning. The creation of a shared vision for how a "dimensionized" system or school site will look and operate is a critical starting point for successful implementation. When staff are empowered to help create that vision, they are more likely to align themselves with it and use it to guide and inform their professional behavior. The great danger in any innovative program is the temptation to use a top-down process in which all staff are required to receive a generic training that bears little or no connection to their individual and collective sense of purpose.

Transcending the limits of mechanistic thinking in an organization undergoing DoL implementation can be supported through what Senge and others refer to as "mental modeling." Similar to the advanced and graphic organizers encountered in the Dimension 2 training called "teaching for declarative knowledge," mental models are expectations and unconscious pictures that determine how we make sense of the world and, ultimately, how we take action within it.

As teachers encounter the complexities of Dimensions of Learning, they are forced to confront their own mental models about how a classroom should look, how students should be taught, and how power and control should be allocated during the instructional process. In taking into account the inevitable conflicts between a system's vision for DoL and its staff's mental models about how instruction should operate, staff members should be encouraged to observe, discuss, and share how their individual mental models are consistent with—or at odds with—the expressed vision for DoL implementation. As Senge suggests, the following skills can be invaluable in managing the mental models that exist throughout an organization:

- Encouraging staff members to recognize "leaps of abstraction" (i.e., noticing our jumps from observation to generalization).

- Exposing the "left-hand column" (i.e., articulating what we normally do not say).

- Balancing inquiry and advocacy (i.e., skills for honest investigation).

- Facing up to distinctions between espoused theories (what we say) and theories-in-use (the implied theory in what we do) (p. 186).

Diana Smith reminds us that the adult learner does not master an innovation like Dimensions of Learning all at once (in Senge 1990, p. 377). Smith describes a three-stage process for developing new capacities that may be helpful in observing the process of implementing Dimensions of Learning:

- **Stage One: New Cognitive Capacities.** People see new things and can speak a new language. This allows them to see more clearly their own and others' assumptions and actions, and consequences of both. Typically, they find it hard to translate these new cognitive and linguistic competencies into fundamentally new actions. They may begin to behave differently, but the basic rules, assumptions, and values are the same.

- **Stage Two: New Action Roles.** As old assumptions loosen in response to the cognitive insights of Stage One, people begin to experiment with action rules based on new assumptions so they can see what they yield. They may need to rely on the new language to produce new actions, and they will find it difficult to access or string together new rules when under stress.

- **Stage Three: Values and Operating Assumptions.** People can string together rules that reflect new action values and operating assumptions. They can enact these rules under stress and ambiguity, continuing to aid their own and others' learning. By this stage, people will have adapted the rules into their own personal model, speaking in their own voice.

Developing and implementing a successful strategic plan for Dimensions of Learning requires sensitivity and attention to the needs of the adult learner, particularly as he or she responds to the demands of a challenging new innovation at his or her work site. Numerous books and articles are currently available on organizational theory, Total Quality Management, and the principles of the learning organization. A brief review of a few of these approaches may be useful in exploring the issue of staff empowerment as it relates to DoL adoption.

In their book, *The Self-Renewing School,* Joyce, Wolf, and Calhoun (1993) emphasize that as we keep student learning central to our efforts to improve the organization of the school, we should also consider the nature of a healthy organization and how to bring it about. In their view, all personnel must become students of school improvement, so that an integrated culture of professionals is developed. Everyone in the system becomes knowledgeable about

- Group decision making,
- Options for staff development,
- Team-generated curriculum,
- Action research for school improvement, and
- Change as a personal and organizational process (p. 22).

Similar principles are evident in Marburger's *One School at a Time: School Based Management—A Process for Change* (1989), Bonstingl's *Schools of Quality: An Introduction to Total Quality Management in Education* (1982), and a wide variety of texts and articles on empowering teachers through peer coaching and action research, including Emily Calhoun's *How to Use Action Research in the Self-Renewing School* (1994) and *Reclaiming the Classroom: Teacher Research as an Agency for Change,* edited by Dixie Goswami and Peter Stillman (1987). Each of these texts underscores the need for collaboration and shared commitment when implementing a complex organizational change element such as Dimensions of Learning.

Essential Planning Questions

What are the essential questions a school or school system might ask itself as it plans for successful Dimensions of Learning implementation? Each site will vary in its needs, commitment, and vision; however, the following list of questions may be helpful in determining areas of inquiry. Also, focus group research may be useful in establishing baseline data at the beginning of the implementation process.

- Is there a *collective vision* articulated for Dimensions of Learning implementation? Have staff reached consensus about its purpose in the school or school system?

- Have the staff reached consensus about the ways in which Dimensions of Learning *aligns with and supports* other major school or school system priorities and initiatives?

- Is there ongoing examination of how the staff will revise *written curriculum* to reflect the essential design elements and principles of the Dimensions of Learning model? How will the system move toward a curriculum that reinforces a *constructivist classroom* that is student-centered, experience-based, and committed to meaningful-use tasks? To what extent have the staff developed and implemented a core curriculum with clearly articulated outcomes that reinforce higher-level thinking skills for all students?

- Have administrators planned for *ongoing professional development* for all relevant staff members, to ensure that they understand the program and can articulate how they will translate it into practice in their own programs and disciplines?

- How are staff modifying the school or school system's approach to *assessing and evaluating student progress* in light of Dimensions of Learning design principles? To what extent is there evidence that staff will increasingly emphasize performance-based assessment models, instruments, and strategies?

- How are *all levels of the school system*, including the members of the Board of Education, engaged in the Dimensions of Learning implementation process?

- To what extent have the Board and administrators obtained *financial support* to ensure successful long-term implementation, rather than short-term, quick-fix approaches often encountered in unsuccessful staff development initiatives?

- How are staff planning for the *needs of the adult learner* and the major phases of the *change process*?

As staffs at both the school site and system levels explore how to create a learning organization during the implementation process, they may also wish to use the questionnaires included at the end of this chapter. Grouped under the heading "Observing the Dimensions of Learning Implementation Process at a School Site," these three questionnaires are arranged according to levels of specificity.

Questionnaire 1, "Dimensions of Learning and School Philosophy" (Figure 2.1 on page 15), can be used by staffs during the early phase of program adoption. They may wish to use this as an entry-level means of assessing the extent to which the philosophy and research underlying the program are already evident in their school.

Questionnaire 2, "An Overview of the Five Dimensions of Learning" (Figure 2.2 on page 16), can assist staffs in planning for initial adoption of the Dimensions of Learning model. School teams can use this instrument to evaluate the extent to which specific design principles for each of the five dimensions are currently operative at their school site.

Finally, Questionnaire 3, "Dimensions of Learning Strategies and Interventions" (Figure 2.3 on page 18), can assist staffs as they begin the formal process of implementation. As they explore together and individually the diverse strategies and interventions identified for each dimension, they can use this questionnaire to assess the extent to which instructional techniques presented in the program may already be in use in some classrooms and programs. Planning teams wishing to complete a detailed evaluation of their present use in the school can gather aggregate data from this survey to establish a baseline portrait of their school site.

This chapter is designed to introduce and reinforce the concept of the school and the school system as learning organizations. The goal of successful Dimensions of Learning implementation can best be achieved in a climate and culture that empowers staff and encourages them to use their talents and insights to realize collectively the vision of making Dimensions of Learning a reality within the organization. A critical aspect of that process is a shift in the paradigm associated with the observation process, transforming it from the traditional *administrator observes/teacher is observed* model into a rich repertoire of options that includes cognitive and peer coaching and action research. Creating a paradigm shift in the teacher observation process is the major focus of the next chapter, "Observation in Transition."

Figure 2.1
Questionnaire 1:
Dimensions of Learning and
School Philosophy

As school staffs begin to explore the Dimensions of Learning model, they may wish to use the following scale to evaluate the extent to which the philosophy and research underlying the program are already evident in their school.

5	**4**	**3**	**2**	**1**	**0**
Extensively	**Frequently**	**Fairly regularly, but need greater emphasis**	**Occasionally**	**Rarely**	**Never**

_____ 1. An active, student-centered approach to instruction is evident throughout our school, with students encouraged to relate academic learning to the world outside the classroom.

_____ 2. Teachers acknowledge and incorporate students' prior knowledge into day-to-day classroom practice.

_____ 3. Cooperative learning and other strategies that encourage social interaction among students are used in all classrooms.

_____ 4. Teachers operate out of the assumption that learning is closely tied to particular situations; explicit planning and support for transfer of learning to new situations occur in all classrooms.

_____ 5. The curriculum in our school emphasizes explicit teaching of attitudes, perceptions, and mental habits that facilitate learning.

_____ 6. Students learn strategies designed to help them improve their ability to solve problems, make decisions, and think critically.

_____ 7. Creativity is valued and encouraged throughout our school.

_____ 8. We have a stated schoolwide philosophy about the learning process and its relationship to the improvement of students' thinking skills.

_____ 9. Staff members and administrators model productive habits of mind, including self-regulated, critical, and creative thinking.

_____ 10. In our school, student assessment focuses on students' reasoning skills and use of information, rather than on recall of information.

FIGURE 2.2
Questionnaire 2:
An Overview of the Five
Dimensions of Learning

As staffs plan for initial adoption of the Dimensions of Learning model, school-based planning teams can employ the following scale to evaluate the extent to which major features of the program currently operate in the school.

5	4	3	2	1	0
Extensively	**Frequently**	**Fairly regularly, but need greater emphasis**	**Occasionally**	**Rarely**	**Never**

DIMENSION 1: Positive Attitudes and Perceptions About Learning

_____ 1. The learning climate in our school is a positive one.

_____ 2. Teachers help students feel accepted in their classrooms.

_____ 3. Classroom experiences are designed to help students develop a sense of comfort.

_____ 4. Students develop a sense of order and safety because of clear rules, procedures, and policies.

_____ 5. Instructors help students perceive academic tasks as valuable.

_____ 6. Staff members help students believe that they have the ability and resources to perform challenging academic tasks.

_____ 7. Teachers clearly identify and articulate the specific behaviors expected of students before, during, and after completion of tasks.

DIMENSION 2: Acquiring and Integrating Knowledge

_____ 1. All curricula in the school clearly communicate the declarative knowledge (the facts, concepts, generalizations, and principles) and the procedural knowledge (the skills and processes) to be mastered.

_____ 2. Students are clear about the learning outcomes they are expected to achieve.

_____ 3. All classes are designed to help students construct meaning for themselves through the use of interactive strategies such as think-pair-share and KWL (Know/Want to Know/Learned) activities.

_____ 4. Students learn to organize information using such devices as the graphic organizer.

_____ 5. Students learn to store information in long-term memory through the use of mnemonic (memory recall) devices.

_____ 6. When learning new skills and processes, students are first presented with clear models that delineate the steps or components of that skill or process.

_____ 7. Students receive extensive opportunities to practice and shape a skill or process in a variety of settings and situations.

_____ 8. Students demonstrate their ability to use skills and processes spontaneously and effortlessly.

(*continued*)

DIMENSION 3: Extending and Refining Knowledge

_____ 1. Questions posed by teachers concentrate on higher-order thinking skills such as comparison, classification, induction, and deduction, rather than on rote memory or knowledge/recall of information.

_____ 2. Students are encouraged to identify essential questions that they wish to explore in order to extend and refine their learning.

_____ 3. The curriculum clearly identifies the information that students are expected to extend and refine.

_____ 4. Activities are designed to help students extend and refine their knowledge.

DIMENSION 4: Meaningful Use of Knowledge

_____ 1. Culminating activities are provided to help students apply knowledge to settings beyond the classroom.

_____ 2. All units include tasks that are student-directed, experience-based, and long-term in design.

_____ 3. The curriculum clearly identifies the "big issues" to be investigated by students.

_____ 4. Performance assessment, including the use of portfolios, reinforces the authentic nature of students' instructional experiences.

_____ 5. Culminating activities involve tasks requiring extensive student interaction and cooperation.

DIMENSION 5: Productive Habits of Mind

_____ 1. The goals and objectives for instruction in all subjects clearly specify the thinking processes expected of each student.

_____ 2. Students and staff understand and can articulate the mental habits encouraged in the school.

_____ 3. Self-regulated thinking (e.g., monitoring one's own attitudes, effective use of resources, and planning) is encouraged in all classrooms.

_____ 4. Critical thinking (e.g., seeking accuracy, seeking clarity, and restraining impulsivity) is a major part of all instructional experiences.

_____ 5. Students are encouraged to push the limits of their knowledge and abilities through creative thinking.

FIGURE 2.3

Questionnaire 3:
Dimensions of Learning
Strategies and Interventions

As staffs begin to implement the Dimensions of Learning program, they will need to understand and employ a diverse array of strategies and interventions identified for each dimension. Many of the instructional techniques presented in the program may already be in use in some classrooms. Planning teams wishing to complete a detailed evaluation of their present use in the school can employ the following rating scale.

5	4	3	2	1	0
Extensively	**Frequently**	**Fairly regularly, but need greater emphasis**	**Occasionally**	**Rarely**	**Never**

DIMENSION 1: Positive Attitudes and Perceptions About Learning

I. Teachers help students feel accepted by

_____ A. Trying to establish a relationship with each student in the class.

_____ B. Monitoring their own attitudes, including unconscious negative expectations of certain students.

_____ C. Engaging in positive classroom behaviors equally with all students.

_____ D. Providing students with opportunities to engage in cooperative learning activities.

_____ E. Helping students create strategies for gaining acceptance by peers.

II. Teachers help students develop a sense of comfort by

_____ A. Frequently and systematically using activities that involve physical movement.

_____ B. Having students develop personal standards for comfort and order.

_____ C. Working with students on "bracketing"; that is, minimizing the effect of distracting or disturbing thoughts so that students can attend to instructional tasks effectively.

III. Teachers help students develop a sense of order by

_____ A. Establishing and communicating clear classroom rules and procedures.

_____ B. Establishing clear policies about the physical safety of students.

_____ C. Being aware of students who might be victimized or physically threatened by other students inside or outside the class.

IV. Teachers help students develop positive attitudes and perceptions about classroom tasks by

_____ A. Communicating to students the teachers' sense of purpose and excitement about the subject matter they teach, with the goal of helping students develop academic trust.

_____ B. Linking classroom tasks to student interests and goals.

_____ C. Having students generate tasks that apply to their interests and goals.

V. Teachers help students believe that they have the ability and resources to succeed in school by

_____ A. Providing positive feedback.

_____ B. Breaking complex tasks into small steps or parts, when appropriate.

(continued)

DIMENSION 2: Acquiring and Integrating Knowledge

I. Teachers help students to construct meaning for declarative knowledge by

_____ A. Using a three-minute pause while presenting information.

_____ B. Helping students to experience content using a variety of senses.

_____ C. Presenting students with the KWL (Know/Want to Know/Learned) strategy.

_____ D. Using a concept attainment process—allowing students to explore and experience a concept before labeling it, so that they learn the concept inductively.

_____ E. Using reciprocal teaching techniques for reading assignments, including summarizing, questioning, clarifying, and predicting.

_____ F. Presenting students with the Before-During-After strategy for use in acquiring information from reading material and other sources.

II. Teachers help students to organize declarative knowledge by

_____ A. Having students create physical and pictographic representations of information.

_____ B. Having students use graphs and charts.

_____ C. Having students identify organizational patterns and describe them using graphic representations.

_____ D. Providing students with advanced organizer questions.

_____ E. Presenting note-taking strategies that use graphic representations.

III. Teachers help students to store declarative knowledge by

_____ A. Presenting students with the strategy of symbols and substitutions.

_____ B. Presenting students with the link strategy.

_____ C. Presenting students with formal systems for storing information, such as the rhyming pegword system, the number/picture system, and the familiar place system.

IV. Teachers help students to construct models for procedural knowledge by

_____ A. Using think-aloud's to demonstrate a new skill or process.

_____ B. Presenting students with a written set of steps.

_____ C. Having students create flow charts.

_____ D. Having students mentally rehearse the steps involved in a skill or process.

V. Teachers help students to shape procedural knowledge by

_____ A. Demonstrating and providing practice in the important variations of the skills or process.

_____ B. Demonstrating some of the common errors or pitfalls in a skill or process.

_____ C. Having students use essential skills or processes in a variety of situations, with appropriate teacher scaffolding to ensure effective transfer.

VI. Teachers help students to internalize procedural knowledge by

_____ A. Having students set up a practice schedule.

_____ B. Having students chart their accuracy when practicing new skills or processes.

_____ C. Having students chart their speed when learning a new skill or process.

(continued)

DIMENSION 3: Extending and Refining Knowledge

I. Teachers help students to extend and refine knowledge by

_____ A. Asking students extending and refining questions before they engage in learning experiences.

_____ B. Asking students extending and refining questions during learning experiences.

_____ C. Asking students extending and refining questions after they have engaged in learning experiences.

_____ D. Having students identify the extending and refining questions they would like to explore and answer.

II. Teachers help students to extend and refine knowledge by

_____ A. Introducing an essential thinking process to students.

_____ B. Presenting students with steps involved in the process.

_____ C. Providing students with ways of graphically representing the process.

_____ D. Presenting students with teacher-constructed tasks related to the process.

_____ E. Presenting students with student-structured activities related to the process.

_____ F. Presenting students with additional process-based activities.

III. Teachers help students to extend and refine knowledge by applying steps A–F (in Section II above) to each of the following thinking processes:

_____ A. *Comparison*—identifying similarities and differences.

_____ B. *Classification*—categorizing elements according to clearly specified attributes or characteristics.

_____ C. *Induction*—investigating information and drawing inferences and conclusions based on that information.

_____ D. *Deduction*—developing arguments and specific statements from generalizations and principles, including the use of syllogistic reasoning.

_____ E. *Analyzing errors*, including fallacies in reasoning or logic.

_____ F. *Constructing support*, including the development of persuasive arguments.

_____ G. *Abstracting*—identifying general patterns and connections.

_____ H. *Analyzing perspectives*, including biases and values implicit in a reading selection or oral presentation.

DIMENSION 4: Meaningful Use of Knowledge

I. Teachers design curriculum and instructional activities so that students understand the applications of knowledge to the world beyond the classroom by

_____ A. Regularly involving students in extended, student-directed, and experiential learning activities.

_____ B. Encouraging students to understand the purpose and utility of the tasks in which they are engaged.

II. Teachers give students a wide range of experiences that involve the following meaningful-use tasks:

_____ A. *Decision making*, including the use of a coherent model of decision making and its application to "real world" decisions and situations.

_____ B. *Investigation*, including students' exploration of historical events and trends, the evolution of a key concept or definition, and research-based projection about future trends.

_____ C. *Problem solving*, including modeling steps involved in the problem-solving process and experience with unstructured problem tasks.

_____ D. *Experimental inquiry*, including both teacher-structured and student-structured experimental tasks.

(continued)

DIMENSION 5: Productive Habits of Mind

I. Teachers reinforce productive habits of mind by

_____ A. Identifying those mental habits that are essential to success in a subject or discipline.

_____ B. Having students identify situations in which specific mental habits would be useful.

_____ C. Having students develop strategies and techniques to help them use these mental habits.

_____ D. Having students identify and pursue long-term goals related to these mental habits.

_____ E. Appointing process observers to identify examples of specific mental habits used during classroom activities.

II. Teachers encourage students to become self-regulated thinkers by helping them to

_____ A. Be aware of their own thinking.

_____ B. Plan.

_____ C. Be aware of necessary resources.

_____ D. Be sensitive to feedback.

_____ E. Evaluate the effectiveness of their own actions.

III. Teachers encourage students to become effective critical thinkers by helping them to

_____ A. Be accurate and seek accuracy.

_____ B. Be clear and seek clarity.

_____ C. Be open-minded.

_____ D. Restrain impulsivity.

_____ E. Take a position when the situation warrants.

_____ F. Be sensitive to the feelings and level of knowledge of others.

IV. Teachers encourage students to demonstrate creative thinking by helping them to

_____ A. Engage intensely in tasks even when answers or solutions are not immediately apparent.

_____ B. Push the limits of their knowledge and abilities.

_____ C. Generate, trust, and maintain their own standards of evaluation.

_____ D. Generate new ways of viewing a situation outside the boundaries of standard conventions.

3

Observation in Transition

We are in the midst of a revolution in teacher observation practices. The old and increasingly outworn model of observation typically involved a mechanistic transaction in which an administrator assumed the hat of "expert" and the teacher assumed the subordinate and passive role of "the observed." Using an approach that usually involved a checklist of teacher/student interactions, the observer examined the teaching episode for a discrete set of atomistic behaviors. During post-observation conferences, the teacher essentially listened to the administrator's list of observation data and conclusions. Instead of a meaningful interaction involving shared inquiry, the exercise was a top-down critique of the teacher's behavior.

During the last decade, we have seen a virtual explosion of new models and practices due to breakthroughs in the fields of cognitive research, learning theory, and organization development. These breakthroughs have led to the development of cognitive coaching, peer coaching, and action research, all extensions of the clinical supervision approach.

The process of clinical supervision, formally introduced in the late 1960s and early 1970s by Robert Goldhammer and Morris Cogan, is committed to empowering the teacher through a transformation of the observation process. Goldhammer (1969), Cogan (1973), and their colleagues emphasize that the teacher-practitioner must be an active participant in the observation of his or her own classroom.

Using a cyclical approach involving pre-observation planning and conferencing, observing, and post-observation conferencing, Goldhammer and Cogan strongly recommend that the teacher have direct input into what will be observed. In effect, the teacher retains the locus of control, guiding and informing the process by identifying key areas in which he or she wants input for improving instruction and student performance. According to Cogan, clinical supervision produces teachers who can analyze their own performance, are open to help from others, and are self-directed.

Three variations and extensions of the clinical supervision model offer particular promise for schools and school systems implementing Dimensions of Learning. These models—cognitive coaching, peer coaching, and action research—offer rich opportunities for educators using Dimensions of Learning. All three of these interrelated approaches to observation reinforce the following features of an effective learning organization:

- An organization will improve only if individual practitioners are actively involved in the improvement process rather than passively removed from it.

- The acquisition of new knowledge is the result of active engagement of the learner. If teachers are to model productive mental habits for their students (i.e., self-regulated, critical, and creative thinking), those habits must be fostered whenever instructional and curriculum innovations are introduced and reinforced.

- Educational innovations can never become fully operational unless practitioners are encouraged and trained to support one another in their use. Coaching experiences, rather than traditional forms of passive observation, are critical to the success of meaningful, long-term organizational change.

- Becoming a learning organization requires all members of the organization to function successfully as a team. Through ongoing opportunities for coaching and site-based action research, the full power of team synergy can be achieved.

Cognitive coaching is the term used by Costa and Garmston (1994) for a nonjudgmental set of practices built around a planning conference, lesson observation, and a follow-up reflective conference. In creating a learning organization, cognitive coaching can become the operative framework for guiding and informing all facets of the observation process. It delineates a set of fundamental assumptions, principles, and skills that can function in both formal and informal interactions with faculty, students, and parents.

Peer coaching is one form of cognitive coaching. At its heart is a commitment to the empowerment of teachers by providing them with the time and resources to become a collaborative support system for one another through shared observation, planning, and program development.

The ultimate extension of peer coaching is a process growing nationally in both power and popularity called *action research*. Through a process of shared inquiry, reflection, and decision making, school-based staffs can become research teams committed to identifying and solving the inevitable problems and issues that will surface from a major change variable like the Dimensions of Learning implementation process.

Used separately, each of these processes can complement and enhance meaningful Dimensions of Learning adoption and implementation. Used in tandem, they can revolutionize a school's operations, greatly expanding the chances that it will become a true learning organization.

Cognitive Coaching and Observing for Dimensions of Learning

According to Costa and Garmston (1994), cognitive coaching is organized around three essential goals: (1) establishing and maintaining *trust*, an assured reliance on the character, ability, or strength of someone or something; (2) facilitating *mutual learning*, the engagement and transformation of mental processes and perceptions; and (3) enhancing growth toward *holonomy*, a characteristic of learning organizations in which individuals act autonomously while also acting interdependently with the group. Ultimately, they suggest, the goal of cognitive coaching is mutual learning for both the teacher and his or her coach.

The critical relationship between Dimensions of Learning and cognitive coaching stems from their agreement that learning is a constructed and active process, rather than a passive, receptive one. True learning, the two models suggest, must incorporate the learner's background knowledge and experience. It must also allow for shared inquiry. Teaching is not a one-sided, mechanistic delivery of discrete instructional behaviors; instead, it involves the teacher-practitioner and the student-participant in a process of dialogue and transaction.

Just as Dimensions of Learning stresses the need for the learner to metacognitively process, in an ongoing way, what and how she is learning, the teacher and cognitive coach require time to explore the inner thought processes and intellectual functions that underlie the teaching process being observed. In effect, the cognitive coaching process allows the teacher to identify and expand his or her mental maps, as Senge calls them—the inner thoughts that are related to various aspects of the teaching act.

Costa and Garmston believe that the effective cognitive coach must function both as a facilitator of learning and as a mediator of the process. For example, in a cognitive coaching session that explores issues related to Dimension 3, extending and refining learning, the cognitive coach must diagnose and envision desired stages for implementing key strategies and techniques related to that dimension, as well as the instructional setting within which they will be observed. The coach needs to construct and use clear and precise language to facilitate the teacher's cognitive development as it relates to Dimension 3 techniques, strategies, and processes.

Perhaps most importantly, the effective cognitive coach must be able to devise a viable overall strategy through which individuals can move themselves toward desired cognitive and instructional operations. Finally, the cognitive coach must commit to assisting the teacher in moving toward more independent, autonomous states of mind and behavior. Costa and Garmston emphasize that the effective cognitive coach needs to believe in his or her capacity to be a catalyst for the growth of the individual(s) being coached.

The materials in this book, including a wide variety of models and examples for post-observation feedback related to each of the five dimensions of learning, can be used by a coach responsible for mediating the observation process. These materials are intended as guideposts for training, rather than as prefabricated or preformed comments to be slotted into a written observation form.

It is crucial that the Dimensions of Learning cognitive coach have internalized the model and constructed meaning around it from using it in his or her own professional practice. In addition, when coaching another educator in the use of Dimensions of Learning tactics and interventions, the cognitive coach needs to consider the context or learning environment in which these strategies will be employed.

Costa and Garmston (1994, p. 17) suggest that a cognitive coach pose the following questions as part of the observation process:

- Where does this lesson fit into the teacher's overall, long-range plan for students? What has happened previously in relationship to this technique or process?

- Is there essential information about the social dynamics of the class I will be observing that I should know?

- Do I need to know any specific behavioral information about the class as a whole or about specific students in it?

- Are there aspects of the lesson, and the Dimensions of Learning techniques and strategies to be used, about which the teacher is unclear or would like particular input?

- Are there specific concerns about trying out or reinforcing a particular Dimensions of Learning strategy or technique in this lesson?

- Are there circumstances or events beyond the classroom experience that may be affecting student performance?

The cognitive coaching process can assume a variety of forms. Generally, however, it involves four essential phases or components: (1) *planning*, in which the coach encourages the teacher to clarify lesson outcomes, identify DoL teaching strategies and decisions, determine evidence of student achievement, and identify the focus of data gathering and procedures that relate to the components to be observed; (2) *teaching*, in which the coach observes the teaching episode and gathers evidence related to the use of the previously identified strategies, as well as their impact on student achievement; (3) *reflecting*, in which the coach asks the teacher to summarize impressions and assessments of the lesson and its DoL components, recall data to support those impressions and assessments, compare planned versus actual teacher and student performances, and draw conclusions about ways the instructional decisions affected student achievement of desired outcomes; and (4) *applying*, in which the coach encourages the teacher to synthesize what he or she has learned about DoL strategy implementation, identify future modifications and applications, and reflect on the coaching process, including recommendations for refinement.

Peer Coaching and Observing for Dimensions of Learning

Cognitive coaching is frequently used in situations where a teacher is being observed by an administrator or instructional supervisor. However, it is equally adaptable to the process of peer coaching, in which teachers coach one another in the use of Dimensions of Learning techniques and strategies. Unlike the more typical, formal observation process involving administrator and teacher, peer coaching can involve coaching dyads or groups of practitioners who work together to facilitate instructional change through the power and synergy of the team process.

From the beginning, Dimensions of Learning has emphasized the value of peer study teams. The essence of peer coaching, for example, is clearly reflected in the "Guidelines for Study Team Success" presented in *Implementing Dimensions of Learning* (Marzano et al. 1992b), which suggests that effective study teams exemplify

- Both autonomy and accountability.
- An emphasis on both relationships and tasks.
- Designated leadership and shared leadership.
- A focus on the impact of instructional decisions on student work.
- The development of a set of working norms to guide both group development and attention to task.
- The demonstrated support of the principal, especially through attendance at study team meetings.
- Agreed-upon communication mechanisms both within the group and in the group's relationship to the school and the district at large.
- A process by which teachers transfer their learnings to the classroom.

In its broadest sense, peer coaching allows teachers to work together in a confidential setting to explore and reflect on the design principles, components, and strategies or processes that make up the Dimensions of Learning program. Study teams of peer counselors are particularly useful in helping teachers observe and evaluate the extent to which DoL practices already operate within their classrooms or can become operative with minor modifications, shared resources, and collegial support.

One-to-one and small-group peer coaching can be used to help team members to expand, refine, or build new Dimensions of Learning instructional skills and techniques. Team members can teach one another, particularly in non-threatening, risk-free team meetings where both successful and unsuccessful attempts at trying out new strategies can be shared and evaluated. Using the power of group synergy, peers can also coach one another through complex problem-solving and decision-making processes related to key aspects of Dimensions of Learning implementation.

As the videotape series *Opening Doors: An Introduction to Peer Coaching* (ASCD 1991c) shows, practitioner/coach interactions can assume a variety of functions and levels of analysis. Educators new to the process, for example, might wish to support one another to improve instruction and enhance team building through *mirroring*, a process in which the coach records but does not interpret the data the teacher has requested. *Collaborative coaching*, on the other hand, is particularly useful in making sure that training transfers from workshop to classroom practice. Through this process, the practitioner and the coach work together to find ways to improve teaching. Finally, *expert coaching* can be used to capitalize on the expertise and knowledge of site-based staff members or specialists from outside the school. In this form of action research, the coach acts as a mentor, giving direct and specific feedback to teachers to assist them in improving instruction and student performance.

Perhaps most importantly, peers observing peers can mutually reinforce a key principle underlying the acquisition of Dimension 2 procedural knowledge skills—namely, that a skill or procedure can become a part of an individual's repertoire only through ongoing opportunities to practice it in a variety of situations and settings. No procedural knowledge acquisition occurs easily or effortlessly. By providing both cognitive coaching and peer support and encouragement, an effective peer coach can assist another teacher in working through the rough spots and inevitable problems that accompany the use of any new strategy or intervention.

The goal of peer coaching is to reinforce the ability of the teacher-practitioner to function as a member of a learning organization. Through peer coaching in pairs and in study teams, teachers can successfully provide one another technical, reflective, and research support to sustain the implementation process. As Pam Robbins suggests in *How to Plan and Implement a Peer Coaching Program* (1991), effective peer coaching can contribute significantly to the creation of a learning organization. It can reduce teacher isolation, build norms that enable teachers to give and receive ideas and assistance, and create a forum for addressing instructional problems. As Joyce and others (1993) affirm, it is the only real basis for ensuring that skills learned in training and other forms of professional development are transferred successfully to the classroom.

Action Research and Observing for Dimensions of Learning

When peer coaching dyads and teams formalize their approach to problem solving and decision making related to Dimensions of Learning implementation, they are moving toward adopting the process of action research. The challenge of effective DoL adoption and implementation can center around the investigation of the following action research questions:

- How do we decide which aspects of the Dimensions of Learning program to implement first?

- How do we guide and inform our decision-making process with real data about our students and their performance within our existing instructional program, rather than basing our decisions on subjective impressions?

- Which problem-solving steps should we take first?

Through the action research process, schools can fully access the power of the staff as a community of learners and collaborative inquirers. By becoming a Dimensions of Learning action research team, the entire staff, or key members of it, can provide powerful assistance to the school improvement process. Like peer coaching and cognitive coaching, the parameters of action research may vary, depending on the experience, background, and needs of the professionals using the process. The following components, however, appear to be action research universals, as presented in the videotape series *Action Research: Inquiry, Reflection, and Decision Making* (ASCD 1995):

1. *Selecting a Focus*: Reaching agreement about the area of student learning to be addressed by Dimensions of Learning adoption and implementation.

2. *Collecting Data*: Examining various ways to gather objective data about learners and their learning environments—e.g., professional literature; existing sources of data, including grades, attendance, and student records; and new sources of data from surveys, portfolios, and other instruments.

3. *Organizing Data*: Sorting and categorizing information in such a way that it becomes meaningful to everyone involved in the decision-making process.

4. *Analyzing and Interpreting Data*: Using acquired data to inform decisions about students' learning behaviors and attitudes, as well as about the learning environment as it relates to the design principles and program features of Dimensions of Learning.

5. *Taking Action*: After collecting, analyzing, and interpreting the data, relating it to the original DoL goal of creating a strategic plan that will lead to improved student and organizational performance.

Used in isolation, cognitive coaching, peer coaching, and action research can greatly enhance the performance of both the individual practitioner and the study group. Used together, these processes can transform the school and the school system as it moves through the process of implementing Dimensions of Learning. In the following chapters, these approaches to observation are applied to each of the dimensions, with specific suggestions for how to tailor the observation process for each of the five major thinking skills. In addition, guidelines and key questions are presented to help teams in schools and school systems identify and work toward desired student behaviors and organizational behaviors that can result from successful adoption of Dimensions of Learning.

4

Beginning with the End in Mind: Observing Dimension 5

What is the purpose of an education? Current literature on educational reform and school restructuring stresses the need to equip students with lifelong meta-skills and mental habits. It is not enough for students to acquire a body of knowledge that they cannot fully understand or use meaningfully. Educators must also help students develop and apply what Dimensions of Learning calls "productive habits of mind."

Ideally, all students should gain proficiency in the domains of self-regulated, critical, and creative thinking. For our graduates to be equipped to handle the demands of a change-dominated, technology-driven society, they must be able to monitor their own comprehension, plan effectively, demonstrate open-mindedness, and push the limits of their knowledge and abilities. In a global economy requiring more knowledgeable workers and a world in which change is a constant, it becomes an absolute necessity for students to acquire and use rigorous intellectual habits.

School-based staffs and school systems exploring ways to integrate the five dimensions into their observation process would do well, as Stephen Covey reminds us in *The 7 Habits of Highly Effective People* (1990), to begin with the end in mind and consider Dimension 5 as their starting point. As part of this exploration, they will need to consider the following key issues:

- What can we observe in a learning organization such as a school or school system that successfully incorporates productive habits of mind into its daily operations and its long-range strategic planning process?

- What can we observe students knowing and doing in a school setting or classroom that successfully reinforces productive habits of mind?

- How can clinical supervisors, cognitive and peer coaches, and action research teams support teachers' ability to reinforce students' acquisition and use of productive habits of mind?

This chapter explores these issues from multiple vantage points. It begins with a discussion of what should be empirically evident in a learning organization that has been successful in addressing and institutionalizing productive mental habits. How, for example, do employees in such an organization interact? What kinds of governance and management systems operate there? What should we be able to see in daily practice when we walk through the halls?

The chapter, then, examines the issue of observable student behaviors in a classroom or school that is successful in teaching for productive habits of mind. For example, how are metacognitive practices a regular part of students' educational experiences? What should we be able to see in an elementary, middle, or high school setting in which students are self-regulated, critical, and creative in their thinking? Action research is then considered from the perspective of how collaborative site-based research teams can explore and address key issues, problems, and decisions extending from Dimension 5 implementation. Finally, the chapter explores how the formal observation process (including pre-observation conferencing, observing, and post-observation conferencing) can help teachers implement Dimension 5. It considers how clinical supervisors and cognitive and peer coaches can work with teachers to improve students' acquisition of productive mental habits.

Dimension 5 and the Learning Organization

The essence of the learning organization, as Peter Senge emphasizes in *The Fifth Discipline* (1990), is metanoia, the collective ability of an organization to learn and grow in order to achieve its goals and increase its productivity. It is clear that the effective learning organization must embody productive mental habits in all facets of its operations. But what exactly are the mental habits that characterize such an organization? What evidence would demonstrate that an organization practices self-regulated, critical, and creative thinking? What specifically should we be able to observe in a school or school system that consistently practices productive mental habits?

The literature on school reform, school-based management, restructuring, Total Quality Management, and organizational development contains a wide variety of suggestions in answer to these questions. Among the ideas contained in the literature, several themes recur:

- An effective learning organization expresses a commitment to the Total Quality Management principle of continuous progress and continuous improvement.

- Members of an effective learning organization operate in cross-functional teams to solve problems and make decisions. Old bureaucratic lines of division and demarcation are modified to favor organizational patterns that support the talents, contributions, and performance of educators directly involved with a key issue, problem, or decision.

- A focus on process and shared inquiry is evident throughout all parts of the learning organization; ends and means are integrated rather than separated.

- Role descriptions are secondary to a commitment to working together to achieve designated outcomes; teachers and administrators are collegial partners rather than adversaries.

- The successful learning organization always keeps its customer in mind. In both schools and school systems, students and parents should be the ultimate concern and focus of an effective learning organization, rather than secondary to issues of bureaucratic policy and institutional survival.

In the United States today, many state and local reform initiatives reflect these principles. The Maryland State Department of Education (MSDE), for example, describes eight essential indicators of what it calls "School-Based Instructional Decision Making" (SBIDM). Embedded in these indicators is the recognition that staffs must practice productive mental habits in their school improvement planning—habits such as being *self-regulated* (self-aware, committed to effective long-range planning and effective use of available resources, sensitive to both internal and external data-based feedback, and ready to modify their own actions based on self-evaluation); *critical* (committed to accuracy and clarity, open-minded, sensitive to the input of key stakeholders, and strategic rather than reactive in their planning and development); and *creative* (dedicated to pursuing answers to complex and, at times, seemingly insoluble problems and difficult decisions; willing to push the limits of their collective knowledge and abilities; and committed to generating new, more viable ways of viewing and doing things within the school site).

The eight SBIDM indicators are highly congruent with the mental habits and long-term processes required for effective Dimensions of Learning implementation. According to MSDE, school improvement teams must collaboratively plan for changes needed in the schools' curriculum and instructional programs. They must provide leadership in analyzing student performance results and in planning for, and reaching agreement with, school staffs regarding appropriate instructional methods, strategies, and curriculum modifications. Improvement teams, including action research groups, should involve the school and central office staffs, parents, and community members in their discussions and planning activities.

Meaningful analysis and use of data is also essential to the process. School personnel and other stakeholders must interpret and use aggregated (whole group) and disaggregated (broken down according to significant subgroups such as race, ethnicity, and gender) performance data generated from the state and local data-based areas. Across departments and across grade levels, school staffs should frequently discuss school and student performance results, progress, and needs.

Ultimately, a school improvement plan that focuses on student outcomes should serve as a blueprint for action by all those providing services to students in the building. Based on goals included in the plan, teachers directly assist students in improving their performance in identified areas, as well as their long-term educational and employment options. Equally important, school improvement teams continuously monitor the long- and short-term impact of the improvement plans and adjust the plans accordingly.

Both the school and the school system can begin to review the extent to which Dimension 5 has become a meaningful part of their learning organization by collectively investigating answers to the following questions:

- To what extent have we clearly articulated the mental habits that we value and are committed to helping students acquire as a result of participating in our instructional program?

- How have we communicated to students, parents, and community members the specific mental habits that we value and that we work to ensure all students acquire?

- To what extent can our instructional and administrative staffs identify and use a common language to describe the habits of mind that we value and reinforce in our learning organization?

- How do we model and practice self-regulated, critical, and creative thinking in all facets of our learning organization (e.g., long-range planning, meeting behavior, student/staff interactions, etc.)?

- In what ways do we create school norms that place a high value on collaboration and lifelong learning as part of our collective commitment to reinforcing productive mental habits?

- How does our written and taught curriculum reinforce students' development of self-regulated, critical, and creative thinking?

- How does our school improvement planning process encourage staff collaboration and the application of productive habits of mind to shared decision-making and problem-solving processes?

- How successfully have we trained *all* of our staff, including instructors, curriculum specialists, and administrators, in the application of Dimension 5 principles, strategies, and concepts?

- To what extent have we modified our collective approach to assessment and program evaluation to ensure that we can monitor student progress in acquiring productive habits of mind?
- What concrete data do we have to confirm that we are accomplishing our expressed goals and objectives related to productive habits of mind?

The opportunities for a learning organization to use Dimension 5 as a framework to evaluate its progress in achieving continuous improvement and in practicing Senge's concept of metanoia are almost limitless. As a starting point, schools and school systems may wish to translate the language of Dimensions of Learning into icons and curriculum support materials that can be used with all staff members.

On the following pages are several examples of how educators in one school system, the Prince George's County Public Schools in Maryland, transformed Dimension 5 ideas into user-friendly classroom materials. Such a process has two key advantages. It ensures that participants "own" Dimension 5, and it ensures that Dimensions of Learning becomes an organic part of daily practice, rather than a program superimposed from outside.

The first set of materials was generated by a group of elementary school teachers in a state-approved workshop on Dimensions of Learning. They agreed that they wanted to translate the program's descriptions of productive habits of mind to make them more accessible to their students. The result is the "Student-Friendly Self-Assessment Checklists for Productive Habits of Mind" found in Figure 4.1 on p. 41.

The second set of materials (Figure 4.2) was created by Marjorie Klapper of Bladensburg High School. As part of a site-level Dimensions of Learning implementation team, Ms. Klapper used her artistic talents to create a series of poster icons that are now displayed throughout the school. According to the staff, these icons have become convenient reference points for teachers, administrators, and students. They also reinforce a schoolwide commitment to helping students develop self-regulated, critical, and creative thinking. Figure 4.2 on page 42 shows a few samples of these icons.

Observing Student Behaviors Extending from Successful Dimension 5 Implementation

What should we be able to observe in a school that has successfully implemented Dimension 5? What kinds of student behaviors should be evident if a classroom or school has facilitated the development of productive mental habits? The ultimate purpose of an effective Dimensions of Learning program is to produce a lifelong learner, a student who has the cognitive and intellectual resources to be self-regulated, critical, and creative in all facets of his or her life and thinking.

An effective start-up activity is to ask training participants to articulate their individual and collective vision for a thinking school. In evaluating the extent to which their current site approximates that vision, participants might explore the following key questions:

1. As we observe students in classrooms, hallways, lunchrooms, and enrichment and extracurricular activities, what evidence can we find of self-regulated, critical, and creative thinking?

2. How are the students we observe displaying behaviors that suggest they are self-regulated in their thinking? To what extent can we say they

- Are aware of their own thinking and that of others, demonstrating the ability to describe the reasoning processes underlying that thinking?

- Use a coherent planning process, including a clear approach to goal setting and time management?

- Identify and access necessary resources, including managing available resources and finding alternatives if necessary?

- Use feedback to monitor their thinking behaviors, including changing that behavior when the situation warrants it?

- Can evaluate the effectiveness and consequences of their own actions, including assessing the extent to which identified goals were achieved and creating alternative approaches for improving future performance?

3. How are the students we observe displaying behaviors that suggest they are effective critical thinkers? To what extent can we say they

- Strive for accuracy in their thinking, including identifying inaccuracies in their own thinking and in that of other individuals and sources?

- Are committed to being clear in their own thinking and seeking clarity in information presented to them?

- Display open-mindedness, with a willingness to consider ideas contrary to their current opinions and to analyze the validity of their own thinking as well as that of others?

- Restrain impulsivity, including consistent evidence of stopping to think about what they are doing before engaging in complex tasks and stopping to think about their answers before responding to complex questions?

- Are willing to take a position when the situation warrants it, including the ability to identify when their position on an important matter is not being expressed? In such instances, does the student present a contrasting position in an appropriate manner?

- Display sensitivity to the feelings and level of knowledge of others, changing comments or behavior when they recognize they are negatively affecting others?

4. How do students demonstrate creativity in their classrooms and other parts of their learning environment? What evidence can we cite that they

- Have the ability and commitment to engage in tasks when answers or solutions are not immediately apparent?

- Push the limits of their own knowledge and abilities, showing a willingness to pursue challenging and complex goals?

- Generate and maintain personal standards of evaluation for work habits and products they create?

- Produce new ways of viewing a situation outside the boundaries of standard conventions, including the ability to modify their behavior when they realize that their view of the situation is impeding progress?

Clinical supervisors, cognitive and peer coaches, and action research teams may wish to consider these student behaviors and outcomes when exploring how best to support individual teacher and systemwide implementation of Dimension 5. These guiding questions also offer a useful entry point for teams interested in pursuing site-based research projects, the topic of the next section of this chapter. As suggested previously, the ultimate purpose of effective action research is to diminish the effects of organizational problems that may impede student performance. There is no more powerful and dramatic focus for the improvement of student performance than the issue of how to enhance students' productive mental habits.

The Action Research Process and Dimension 5

A site-based action research team facing the challenge of implementing Dimension 5 can explore a wide variety of issues and approaches. In seeking to develop productive habits of mind, the team might consider the following questions to guide and inform their action research process:

- Which mental habits do we wish to emphasize in our instructional program?

- Which mental habits will we introduce?

- How will we reinforce the mental habits?

- How will we train instructional staff and administrators to effectively implement Dimension 5?

- How will we restructure or reorganize our use of written curriculum and supported curriculum (textbooks, software, schedules, etc.) to reinforce students' development of the mental habits we identify as our school's priorities?

- How will we involve students, parents, and community members in the process of identifying and reinforcing essential habits of mind as a schoolwide priority?

- What assessment and evaluation data will we obtain and analyze to determine how our students are acquiring and using the mental habits we identify as our schoolwide commitment?

- As we disaggregate our data to identify potential patterns among particular gender, racial, and/or ethnic groups, how will we provide meaningful support and intervention if individuals or groups are not progressing satisfactorily?

- How will we monitor ourselves as members of a learning organization? How do we ensure that we are all modeling the habits of mind we have identified?

- How will we integrate Dimension 5 into our teacher observation and peer coaching processes?

With these questions as a starting point, the action research team will want to focus on one or more aspects of student progress related to Dimension 5. The team may wish to use the following action research planning model, a five-phase process identified by Calhoun and Glickman (1993):

1. Selecting a Focus. What are our specific areas of concern about students' mastery of one or more of the mental habits we are emphasizing at our school? What are our individual and collective perceptions about why these are areas of concern? What preliminary evidence can we share to help us narrow and discern a focus for our action research process? How can we frame our concern(s) in the form of one or more essential research questions that we can investigate as a team? What justification can we give the rest of the staff to explain our selection of a focus area for this process?

2. Collecting Data. From what sources can we collect objective data about our students' performance in relationship to the focus area we have chosen? For example, if the action research team chooses to investigate student performance related to key components of the mental habit of critical thinking, how might the team acquire concrete data about students' ability to seek accuracy, seek clarity, be open-minded, and restrain impulsivity? As a starting point, what does the professional literature reveal about the chosen focus area? What do disaggregated school-based and system-level data reveal? What might we learn about students' acquisition and use of the mental habits we are investigating through such data sources as staff surveys, observations, anecdotal records, portfolio assessments, and student performance on meaningful-use tasks?

3. Organizing Data. How do we sort and categorize the information we acquire through our data collection process? How do we make sure this information is meaningful to key stakeholders, including faculty and administrative representatives, parents, and community members? Have we acquired sufficient objective, concrete data to begin making decisions about how we will respond to the action research question(s) we have chosen as our focus?

4. Analyzing and Interpreting Data. As we begin to draw conclusions about the data we have collected, what kinds of data analysis procedures will we employ? How will we make sure that our conclusions are valid and appropriate? As we generate preliminary interpretations, how can we make certain that the inferences and recommendations we produce are as comprehensive and valid as possible? How will we corroborate our interpretations and conclusions with key stakeholders beyond our action research team?

5. Taking Action. Based on our data collection, analysis, and interpretation process, what final conclusions and recommendations can we make in response to our original action research question(s)? What are the essential components of the strategic plan we will share with the rest of the staff to execute the decisions we have made as a result of the process? How will we identify and justify recommendations concerning the following elements of our strategic plan:

- Major goals and objectives
- Recommended strategies
- Relevant activities extending from identified strategies
- Individuals and groups responsible for identified activities
- Time line/implementation plan
- Milestones/benchmarks: key points in our implementation process that will be used to generate data concerning student and program progress toward achieving specific objectives
- Evaluation plan explicitly tied to identified outcomes
- Management plan

Through the use of this action research process, school-based planning teams can contribute significantly to the effectiveness of the Dimension 5 implementation process. Site-based action research projects designed to help students develop productive mental habits can also become important parts of a broader research base at the system level, leading to break-throughs in curriculum and instruction, assisting in the creation of more positive learning environments, and guiding districtwide efforts at continuous improvement.

Dimension 5 and the Teacher Observation Process

In observing for Dimension 5, clinical supervisors and cognitive and peer coaches are acquiring data in response to the following questions:

- How does the instructor model self-regulated, critical, and creative thinking?
- How does the instructor encourage students to monitor and evaluate the processes and outcomes of their thinking and actions?
- How does the instructor encourage critical thinking through emphasizing accuracy, clarity, open-mindedness, and restraint of impulsivity?
- How does the instructor encourage creativity in his or her classroom, including situations outside the boundaries of standard conventions?
- How successfully do students demonstrate productive habits of mind?

Within this domain, the clinical supervisor or cognitive or peer coach is responsible for working with teachers on what is perhaps the most complex of the five dimensions of learning. Two caveats are particularly appropriate here: first, make sure that the observer and the instructor are in clear agreement about the specific teacher and student behaviors that are to be observed and, second, be certain there is consensus about the approach the observer will use.

If the clinical supervisor or cognitive coach is asked to help teachers improve their skill in facilitating students' self-regulated thinking, will the observer be examining that mental habit in its entirety or looking at its discrete subcomponents? For example, will the observer assess the ways in which teachers help students become aware of their own thinking, encourage students to plan and use appropriate resources, support students in being sensitive to feedback, or assist students in evaluating the consequences of their own actions? Similarly, will the observer be expected to *mirror* (record but not interpret the observation data requested by teachers), *collaboratively coach* (work in partnership with teachers to improve their facilitation of the habit or its subcomponents), or *provide expert input* (with the supervisor or coach functioning as a mentor, providing specific suggestions, including both commendations and recommendations)?

The "Examples of Observation Feedback" in Figure 4.3 (beginning on page 43) are designed to assist clinical supervisors and cognitive and peer coaches in exploring the observation process related to Dimension 5. These examples represent models for writing feedback statements during observation situations and are not intended to be complete in themselves. Rather, they provide a format for generating actual observation comments during live observation experiences.

Although the feedback is written as commendations and recommendations, the teacher and observer can investigate each of the components in a value-neutral way. For example, they might select one bulleted element (e.g., "Throughout the lesson, you helped students learn how to monitor their own comprehension by teaching effective metacognitive strategies") and use it as a springboard for shared exploration. How would each of them operationally define "metacognitive strategies"? In their opinion, what would constitute effective use of such strategies? What is the range of possible metacognitive options available to the teacher? Are there unique aspects of the class to be observed that might make some metacognitive strategies more desirable than others? Are there specific issues or questions concerning metacognition that the teacher might like the observer to focus on and collect data on while observing the lesson?

Ultimately, the clinical supervision process and the complementary processes of cognitive and peer coaching can be effective only if they are an authentic extension of the professional relationship between the observer and the observed. Each partner must be supportive of the other; both should learn and grow as a result of the observation process. Ideally, the material in this chapter will provide a meaningful starting point for integrating Dimension 5 into this cooperative partnership.

FIGURE 4.1
Student-Friendly Self-Assessment Checklists
for Productive Habits of Mind

CREATIVE THINKING

Ask Yourself

1. Were you willing to keep on going even when you were stuck?

2. How did you extend your own prior knowledge or build on what someone else said?

3. Did you keep your goal in mind? How well did you do?

4. Did you recognize problems? How else could it have been done?

Think About

1. Work together to find an answer; stay with it until you find it.

2. Brainstorm until you've run out of ideas.

3. Believe in your ideas and yourself!

4. Create and accept new ways of seeing.

CRITICAL THINKING

Ask Yourself

1. CORRECT: Is it correct?

2. Does it make sense?

3. *Primary:* Are you listening to what everyone has to say?
Intermediate: Are you being open-minded?

4. Did you think before you spoke? Be cool!

5. Did you make a choice? Did you stick with it?

6. Did you respect yourself and others?

Think About

1. Stay focused on task.

2. Organize your thoughts and ask questions to gain more information.

3. Listen without making judgments.

4. Take turns and give everyone a chance.

5. Support your position and compromise when necessary.

6. Respect and encourage one another

SELF-REGULATED THINKING

Ask Yourself

1. What were you thinking that made you say or do that?

2. For Primary: What did you want to do? For Intermediate: What were your short- and long-term goals?

3. What materials do you have or need to accomplish your goals?

4. Did you listen to everyone's ideas? (Listen/Think/Pair/Share)

5. How to you feel about what you did? **Don't forget to celebrate!**

Think About

1. The reason(s) I think this are
_____ .

2. My goal is _____ .
I will accomplish this goal by (Date/Time) _____ .

3. The resources I used are _____
_____ .

4. Things went well when _____
Things did not go well when _____ .

5. Did I meet my goal? Yes____ No____ .
Next time I will _____ .

Figure 4.2
Samples of DoL Poster Icons from Bladensburg High School

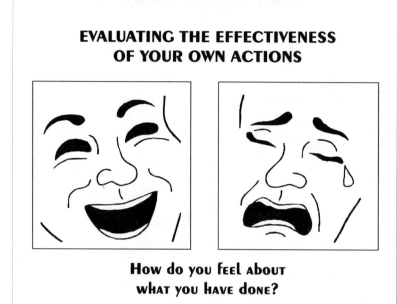

FIGURE 4.3
Dimension 5
Examples of Observation Feedback

I. Helping Students Develop the Mental Habits of Self-Regulation

A. Commendations

- Throughout the lesson, you helped students learn how to monitor their own comprehension by teaching effective metacognitive strategies.

- You encouraged students to plan strategically throughout the lesson.

- You did an excellent job of encouraging students to be aware of resources they could use to complete assigned tasks successfully.

- Through your use of cooperative learning structures and your encouragement of students' self-regulated thinking, you helped them to be sensitive to feedback and use it to modify their behavior.

- Your lesson exemplified the value of helping students assess the effectiveness of their own actions.

B. Recommendations

- Many of your students appeared to experience difficulty in planning, being sensitive to feedback, and evaluating the impact of their actions. You might consider using direct instruction to introduce students to the mental habit of self-regulation and reinforce their use of it.

- Periodically work with students to identify situations in which each of the mental habits of self-regulation would be useful.

- Encourage students to realize that when they are not doing well at a specific task, being aware of their own thinking can help them identify what they are doing wrong.

- Work with your students to develop and use short- and long-range planning skills.

- Explore with students the value of using a variety of sources and materials. Encourage them to analyze independently the range and availability of resources necessary for them to complete required tasks.

- Work with your students to be sensitive to feedback during repetitive tasks, showing how it can help them prevent careless mistakes.

- Help students recognize that when they are doing something new or something they are not very good at, evaluating their actions can help them learn from their mistakes.

- Incorporate opportunities for students to develop strategies and techniques to help them use the mental habits of self-regulation.

- Have students identify and pursue long-term goals; continue to encourage them to relate their education to their identified goals.

- Periodically appoint process observers to identify illustrations of the mental habits of self-regulation during classroom activities.

- Incorporate more metacognitive strategies into your classroom. For example, your students might benefit from think-alouds, reflective journals, mental rehearsals, and related activities to help them monitor their comprehension of material being taught.

(continued)

II. Helping Students Develop the Mental Habits of Critical Thinking

A. Commendations

- You consistently encouraged students to be accurate and seek accuracy.

- By reinforcing students' being clear, seeking clarity, and being open-minded, you encouraged a climate of effective critical thinking in your classroom.

- The discipline evident in your classroom was a clear and positive reflection of your modeling and helping students to internalize the mental habit of restraining impulsivity.

- The discussions and debates you facilitated were powerful reinforcers for students' critical thinking skills, particularly when you encouraged them to take a position that the situation warranted.

- You clearly modeled, and your students reflected, a great sensitivity to the feelings and level of knowledge of others.

B. Recommendations

- Introduce, model, and reinforce students' application of essential critical thinking habits, including their ability to

  – Check themselves along each step of a task or activity.
  – Say what they mean and ask when they don't understand.
  – Listen to other people's ideas.
  – Think first before acting or speaking.
  – Stand up for what they believe while respecting other students' opinions.

- Have students identify situations for which each of the mental habits of critical thinking would be most useful. For example, being clear and seeking clarity is very important if someone is trying to persuade them, if they are trying to explain something to someone else, or if they are not sure about what they are saying or writing.

- Work with students to develop strategies and techniques to help them use the mental habits of critical thinking (i.e., being accurate and seeking accuracy, being clear and seeking clarity, being open-minded, restraining impulsivity, taking a position when the situation warrants, and being sensitive to the feelings and level of knowledge of others).

- Debates are a powerful and effective way to reinforce students' use of critical thinking habits. Please consider incorporating both formal and informal debate into your classroom.

III. Helping Students Develop the Mental Habits of Creative Thinking

A. Commendations

- You did a very effective job of encouraging your students to engage intensely in tasks even when answers or solutions were not immediately apparent to them.

- You consistently helped students to push the limits of their knowledge and abilities.

- Through modeling and rehearsal, you reinforced students' capacity for generating, trusting, and maintaining their own standards of evaluation.

- You did an excellent job of reinforcing students' creativity by encouraging them to generate new ways of viewing situations, outside the boundaries of standard conventions and expectations.

(*continued*)

B. Recommendations

- Students need encouragement and support to test intellectual limits and to develop their creative abilities and imagination. Consider the periodic introduction and reinforcement of important mental habits of creative thinking.

- Work with students to help them articulate and apply mental habits of creative thinking. Such habits might include students' speaking or writing the following affirmations:

  – Hang in there even when the going gets tough!
  – Challenge myself! Don't be afraid to try something new.
  – Know what I want and go for it!
  – Look for new and different ways to approach a task, problem, or decision.
    Explore new ways of dealing with situations. What's something no one else
    has thought of?

- Consider designing some instructional tasks that permit students choice as to approach and final product. This element of the meaningful-use task can help develop students' creativity.

- Have students identify and evaluate examples of creative thinking displayed by peers, themselves, and significant figures from history, literature, film, television, and current events.

- Whenever possible, have students develop techniques and strategies for each of the mental habits of creative thinking, including

  – Engaging intensely in tasks even when answers or solutions are not immediately
    apparent.
  – Pushing the limits of their own knowledge or abilities.
  – Generating, trusting, and maintaining their own standards of evaluation.
  – Generating new ways of viewing a situation, outside standard boundaries.

- Incorporate problem-solving and decision-making activities into your classroom to reinforce students' ability to think creatively.

5

Reinforcing Authenticity in the Classroom: Observing Dimension 4

Dimension 4 is the jewel in the crown of Dimensions of Learning. There is no more effective way for students to apply their productive habits of mind than by engaging in the meaningful-use tasks that constitute Dimension 4. These tasks allow students to take the knowledge they acquire and apply it in meaningful and authentic ways, thus reinforcing the primary purpose of education, to relate classroom learning to the world beyond the school. Ideally, students' education should consist of a variety of meaningful-use tasks that call on students to apply their knowledge to real-life situations involving one or more of the following mental operations:

- Decision making
- Investigation
- Experimental inquiry
- Problem solving
- Invention

A meaningful-use task requires that students assume some form of reality-based role, engage in long-term applications involving one or more of these thinking operations, choose a final product, and participate in a culminating oral presentation or defense of their work. No single lesson can include a complete meaningful-use task; however, a lesson might include either group work or independent work that represents one aspect of completing such a task.

From writing contests to science fair projects, students have opportunities to work on meaningful-use tasks in schools. Write-a-Book activities, film and video contests, and related production-based, long-term projects require that students create a vehicle for expressing themselves, then share their perspectives with the world outside the school setting. In so doing, they become authors, filmmakers, and other real-world identities.

Similarly, when students participate in a science fair, they assumes the role of scientist. Students must formulate a viable hypothesis, then test it by using some form of experimental inquiry. The process of creating their project involves the application and refinement of declarative and procedural knowledge, as well as the use of advanced cognitive skills. Usually, final project presentation involves some form of oral defense in which students discuss with science fair judges their thinking operations and related decision-making steps in designing, implementing, and constructing the project.

Unfortunately, these kinds of experiences are often unavailable to students except on a limited basis during their elementary and high school years. The school or school system that is committed to the ideal of the learning organization and to the goal of teaching effective thinking skills should provide opportunities for students to participate in meaningful-use tasks in all subject areas at all grade levels. In pursuing these goals, school-based staffs and school systems need to consider the following guiding questions:

- What should we be able to observe in a learning organization that successfully integrates meaningful-use tasks into all phases of curriculum, instruction, and assessment?

- What can we observe students knowing and doing in a school setting or classroom that successfully reinforces productive habits of mind?

- How can clinical supervisors, cognitive and peer coaches, and action research teams support teachers' ability to reinforce students' acquisition and use of productive habits of mind?

The sections that follow explore ways for schools and school systems to begin to operationalize meaningful-use tasks. What kinds of institutional changes, for example, should be observable in a learning organization that is successfully implementing Dimension 4? How will critical aspects of the overall instructional program be transformed if meaningful-use tasks become a significant part of ongoing system operations?

The chapter extends this issue into the domain of student performance. As we observe a school or classroom in which Dimension 4 is a consistent and organic element, what student behaviors should we be able to observe? The chapter then presents the kinds of action research questions regarding Dimension 4 that school-based improvement and investigative teams may wish to explore. Finally, the chapter provides a detailed analysis of the specific issues, commendations, and recommendations that may surface in a clinical supervision or coaching interaction between an observer and a teacher who are examining the use of meaningful-use tasks in a classroom setting.

Dimension 4 and the Learning Organization

At the heart of a learning organization that is successfully implementing Dimension 4 is a commitment to the principle of authenticity. How do we ensure that students see purpose and meaning in all aspects of their instructional experience? How do we help students appreciate the value of their education and its application to their world? A learning organization committed to implementing Dimension 4 will need to consider how the organization currently designs, delivers, and monitors instruction to achieve the desired impact. As part of this exploration, members of the organization may choose to examine the current literature and educational research related to learning theory and cognitive development that underlie the Dimension 4 emphasis on the value of meaningful-use tasks.

As Herman, Aschbacher, and Winters state in *A Practical Guide to Alternative Assessment* (1992), learning involves the creation of personal meaning from new information and prior knowledge. In effect, students construct the knowledge they acquire as they relate new information to existing cognitive schema, rather than receive it passively in predigested chunks. Similarly, learning is generally not a linear progression of discrete skills; instead, it is often a nonlinear, messy process of problem solving.

People perform better when they can gauge how their performance compares to designated standards; thus, effective instructional tasks encourage students to review models and examples from the world beyond the classroom. Because learners need opportunities to accommodate their unique learning styles and attention spans, instructional environments should offer students a selection of. tasks and products to complete.

Perhaps most importantly, students need to know when to use knowledge, how to adapt it, and how to manage their own learning (Herman et al. 1992). Real-world opportunities and simulations both provide useful settings for this process to occur. Because motivation, effort, and self-esteem affect both learning and observable performance, Herman and others strongly recommend that teachers motivate students by giving them real-life tasks and opportunities to connect learning to their personal experiences. They stress that learning has significant social components; group work is valuable and should be designed to enable students to take on a variety of roles.

Each of these design elements is inherent in the Dimensions of Learning meaningful-use task. In exploring effective ways to implement Dimension 4, members of the learning organization might consider the following questions:

- To what extent does our written curriculum incorporate consistent use of meaningful-use tasks in all subjects and at all grade levels? To what extent have we successfully eliminated an overloaded curriculum in favor of a core curriculum that allows teachers the time needed to engage students in independent work on authentic, self-directed activities?

- How do the meaningful-use tasks in our written curriculum reinforce students' ability to engage in independent, long-term applications of such meta-skills as decision making, problem solving, experimental inquiry, invention, and investigation?

- How does our instructional program ensure that students develop the independent cognitive skills and mental habits they need to succeed in long-term, performance-based instructional tasks?

- To what extent are our written curriculum and instructional programs consistent with current research in education and cognitive psychology?

- How do we make sure that students' meaningful-use task products are displayed and acknowledged throughout the school? For example, are we making effective use of bulletin board and showcase displays, assemblies, award ceremonies, parent visits, and curriculum showcases to reinforce the value we place on meaningful-use tasks?

- Have we made sure that our students have access to a wide variety of supporting resources and materials to complete their meaningful-use tasks, including library media center materials, technology support, and community resources?

- Does our assessment program align with our commitment to the integration of performance-based, meaningful-use tasks into our instructional program?

- Are we making effective use of portfolio assessment to capture students' progress in completing meaningful-use tasks?

- Have we built in mechanisms to monitor students' metacognitive reflections and intellectual progress as they participate in the meaningful-use tasks they are assigned?

- Are we providing effective professional development for our staff, and parent/community training for our parents and guardians, to ensure that there is consensus about the value and purpose of meaningful-use tasks within our instructional programs?

Perhaps most importantly, members of the learning organization need to consider the kinds of student behaviors they expect to observe when teachers effectively employ meaningful-use tasks. How will ongoing participation in such tasks reinforce students' productive mental habits and their perceptions of themselves as learners?

Observing Student Behaviors Consistent with Effective Implementation of Dimension 4

In observing meaningful-use tasks, we should be able to see evidence of students' ongoing use of productive mental habits. When students are working independently to complete complex, independent activities involving one or more of the Dimension 4 meta-processes (problem solving, decision making, experimental inquiry, investigation, and invention), they must use critical thinking, creative thinking, and self-regulated thinking. Long-term, authentic learning activities require students to push the limits of their thinking, generate a wide variety of ways to approach new situations, and internally monitor their progress toward achieving goals they have set for themselves. Throughout the process of completing a meaningful-use task, students must reflect on standards of completeness, accuracy, and effectiveness.

As members of a learning organization explore ways to implement Dimension 4, they should evaluate the extent to which their students are currently participating in long-term, reality-based learning projects. In generating their vision for a "dimensionized" school, educators might consider the student behaviors listed below. To what extent can we observe these kinds of behaviors on a regular basis? What are the barriers or issues we must confront if we wish to see consistent evidence of these behaviors throughout our school programs in the future? What are the success stories we can celebrate? To what extent can we say that *all* of our students demonstrate these behaviors on a regular basis? Consider the following questions as you observe for student behaviors related to successful Dimension 4 implementation:

1. What evidence can we find to confirm that *all* students at *all* grade levels have regular opportunities to participate in meaningful-use tasks that are

- Application oriented, integrating a variety of higher-order thinking skills (e.g., decision making, problem solving, experimental inquiry, invention, investigation)?

- Designed to allow the student to function as a professional, engaging in roles, problems, and issues in reality-based scenarios?

- Long-term, requiring students to work independently and to access resources beyond the classroom?

- Structured to involve student choice, particularly concerning the approach the student will use and the end product(s)?

- Constructed to produce multiple end results, including tangible end products and some form of oral presentation or defense?

2. In what ways are meaningful-use tasks successfully integrated into the content of the curriculum students study, allowing them to concentrate on the "big issues" inherent in a unit?

3. How are students engaged in long-term authentic tasks that require them to apply a coherent decision-making process to an unresolved decision or issue in a study unit? In observing students as they participate in the decision-making process, to what extent can they

- Demonstrate their command of a coherent approach to decision making, including the ability to define a decision question, articulate alternatives, generate evaluation criteria, and apply those criteria to the selection of a final alternative?

- Display accuracy and effectiveness in their thinking while completing a decision-making task? For example, did the student explore appropriate alternatives using significant evaluation criteria? Was his or her final decision an appropriate one, reflecting a consistent application of identified criteria?

4. Where can we observe students engaged in the process of investigation as part of their completion of a meaningful-use task? To what extent can we say that students

- Explore unresolved issues about the defining characteristics or defining features of something (i.e., *definitional investigation*)?

- Explore unresolved issues about how something occurred or why something happened (i.e., *historical investigation*)?

- Explore unresolved issues about what would happen if . . . or what would have happened if . . . (i.e., *projective investigation*)?

- Use a coherent investigative process to develop and articulate in a complete, accurate, and effective way a resolution to the confusions or contradictions about a concept, past event, or hypothetical event?

5. To what extent are students encouraged to generate and test hypotheses about physical and psychological phenomena, using a coherent and consistent form of experimental inquiry? To what extent can we observe students' ability to

- Describe and explain thoroughly what they observe during the process of experimental inquiry?

- Provide accurate and complete explanations for what they observe?

- Make clear predictions?

- Plan and carry out effectively experiments or activities to test their predictions?

- Use appropriate and accurate concepts, facts, and principles to explain the phenomenon they are studying?
- Make sure that the entire process of experimentation that they design and carry out is accurate and effective, tests their stated predictions, and adequately relates to their initial explanations?

6. How are students encouraged to apply a consistent and coherent approach to problem solving to address situations or processes that contain or require some major constraint or limiting condition? Where can we find evidence that *all* students can

- Clearly identify specific goals to be accomplished in problem-solving situations?
- Accurately identify broad constraints or limiting conditions related to an identified problem?
- Generate and accurately articulate a variety of appropriate ways to overcome identified constraints or limiting conditions?
- Select and defend from the alternatives generated the most appropriate solution to an identified problem?

7. Where can we observe students' creativity being fostered and encouraged in meaningful-use tasks that involve the process of invention? How are students encouraged to

- Create ways to improve on existing situations and conditions or to address unmet needs in their environment?
- Clearly articulate specific, rigorous standards or evaluation criteria that their inventions are required to meet?
- Develop and modify initial models or drafts of their proposed inventions as they develop their products?
- Defend the final products of their invention using the criteria or standards they themselves have generated?

8. To what extent can students clearly articulate the purpose of the meaningful-use tasks they are assigned?

9. To what extent can students identify the relationship of the meaningful-use task(s) to the curriculum they are studying?

10. To what extent are students asked to reflect metacognitively on the thinking processes they use while completing a meaningful-use task?

11. How are students evaluated while completing a meaningful-use task? To what extent do they play a direct role in helping to establish evaluation criteria? How are think logs and reflective journals used to complement students' activities during a meaningful-use task?

12. How are the products generated during a meaningful-use task integrated into the assessment and evaluation process? For example, is some form of portfolio assessment used to maintain student-generated materials? Are videotapes of oral presentations and defenses available for inclusion in student portfolios? How are student-generated products displayed and honored throughout the school? Where do we see examples of each of the following:

- Products that report and communicate the process involved in completing the meaningful-use task, and the results of that process:
  - Oral reports
  - Written reports
  - Videotaped reports
  - Newscasts
  - Dramatic enactments
  - Simulations

- Products that represent an artistic, affective, or symbolic aspect of the task:
  - Paintings
  - Sculptures
  - Murals
  - Artifacts
  - Songs
  - Dramatic presentations
  - Dances

Many of these questions provide a basis for action research groups to explore Dimension 4 processes and skills. The issue of how the meaningful-use task can enhance or complement the performance assessment process is a fertile area for collaborative inquiry and research at the school or system level.

The Action Research Process and the Meaningful-Use Task

As schools and school systems explore the increasingly influential field of performance assessment, the action research process offers an effective avenue for developing performance-based instruction and assessment tasks. Through collaborative, site-based inquiry, staffs can successfully address and find solutions to the problems and issues that will likely surface as they shift their assessment paradigm.

Performance-based instruction and performance assessment both reflect many of the design principles of the Dimension 4 meaningful-use task. Essentially, a performance assessment task requires a student to create an answer or product that demonstrates his or her knowledge or skills. The assessment task should be worthwhile and engaging, requiring students to be active participants, not passive selectors of a single right answer. In completing meaningful-use tasks, students must demonstrate their ability to apply their knowledge and skills to reality-based situations and scenarios. This type of experience requires students to successfully complete a clear, logical series of performance-based activities.

In exploring the use of meaningful-use tasks in a school or school system, action research teams might begin with the following questions to guide their selection of a research focus:

1. How successfully does our written curriculum reflect the design principles of the Dimension 4 meaningful-use task?

2. What are the "big issues" in our curriculum around which we might develop meaningful-use tasks?

3. How successfully have we trained our staff in Dimension 4? To what extent can all of our staff articulate and put into effect the essential ideas and processes associated with the design and development of meaningful-use tasks?

4. What barriers or impediments within our school might interfere with our use of meaningful-use tasks as a fundamental part of all students' educational experiences?

5. What data do we have to confirm that our students are progressing in their ability to acquire and apply productive mental habits to the successful completion of meaningful-use tasks?

6. As part of our assessment program, how are we collecting and analyzing both formative and summative data related to student progress in the domains of

- Decision making?
- Investigation?
- Experimental inquiry?
- Problem solving?
- Invention?

7. What does our analysis of disaggregated data reveal about the progress of students at all grade levels in attaining mastery of these outcomes?

8. How can we expand our assessment repertoire to capture the full range of student experiences and progress in completing meaningful- use tasks?

For example, have we made effective use of the portfolio assessment to reflect students' thinking and the breadth of their independent activities while working on meaningful- use tasks?

9. How can we ensure that meaningful-use tasks are a regular and integrated part of our instructional program, rather than artificial add-ons?

10. To what extent can we say that our entire instructional program emphasizes authenticity, encouraging all students to see the value and application of what they learn in relationship to the world around them?

Action research teams can approach these issues in a variety of ways, depending on their orientation and task as a research group. Investigating how to implement Dimension 4 at a school site can involve a variety of focus areas, including curriculum reform, instructional modifications, professional development design, assessment, and such governance/management issues as staff involvement in scheduling, curriculum development, and materials acquisition. Applying Calhoun and Glickman's five-phase model of action research (1993), staffs might approach the process by investigating some of the following questions:

1. Selecting a Focus. What is the specific area of student learning about which we are particularly interested or concerned? For example, when we observe students participating in meaningful-use tasks, do we find evidence of certain weaknesses or deficiencies in their application of such mental habits as self-regulated, critical, and creative thinking? Are there certain meta-processes that some or all of our students appear to have difficulty in applying? For example, to what extent are all of our students proficient problem solvers and decision makers? To what extent can all of our students develop and complete successfully a process of experimental inquiry? Do all of our students show competence in the process of investigation? To what extent do we have evidence of our students' creativity as displayed in ongoing invention activities? Are there certain patterns of strength and weakness related to one or more of these areas?

2. Collecting Data. Once we have selected our focus for this research project, what objective data do we have available? What does the professional literature tell us about how to improve student performance in the focus area we have identified? To what extent do the sources of data we have available provide a complete and accurate picture of how our students are performing in the area we have selected? To what extent should we expand the repertoire of assessment strategies and approaches we use in this area? After a preliminary review of the available data, do we begin to see patterns of student strength and need? For example, is there an overall or aggregate pattern of need in the area of problem solving? Or do we find specific weaknesses in student performance in certain aspects of our curriculum or among certain subgroups within our overall population?

3. Organizing Data. After we have collected the data, how can we arrange it so that our research team, as well as other relevant audiences, can understand it? Have we made sure that we have obtained both quantitative and qualitative data as a basis for our decision-making process? In the case of meaningful-use task and Dimension 4 implementation, we must be certain that we have collected samples of student products and processes. How can we incorporate these artifacts into our data displays and our data analysis process?

4. Analyzing and Interpreting Data. How can we best turn the data we have acquired into diagnostic information? How can we integrate supporting information from professional literature into our analysis and interpretation process? In addressing a critical aspect of Dimension 4 implementation, to what extent do our data suggest changes needed in key aspects of our instructional program such as curriculum design, staff development, scheduling and staffing configurations, and assessment?

5. Taking Action. What can we conclude about our students' needs and performance in relationship to our original research focus? What innovations and initiatives should we recommend that we undertake as a research team? What innovations and initiatives would we recommend that our entire school or school system consider? Can we now present an action plan that will strategically describe for our staff how we propose improving our students' performance on key aspects of the Dimension 4 meaningful-use task? As we conclude our initial action research process, what would we recommend as our

- Essential goals and objectives?
- Key tasks related to achieving these outcomes?
- Target dates for completing each task?
- Designated responsibilities and duties?
- Required resources?
- Key milestones or benchmarks for monitoring the progress of our plan's implementation?
- Formative and summative evaluation strategies?

One of the most effective data sources for an action research team focusing on Dimension 4 implementation is the wealth of information and insight provided by teacher observation. The next section of this chapter provides a detailed overview of what can be observed in teachers' classrooms when they are successfully integrating meaningful-use tasks into their instructional program. It also presents a number of recommendations for transforming the classroom into an authentic, reality-based learning environment. These suggestions can be a rich source of inquiry for Dimension 4 action research teams beginning the process of data collection.

Dimension 4 and the Teacher Observation Process

Not every lesson will directly address a specific meaningful-use task. However, all lessons in a unit can and should help students develop the ability to respond successfully to such tasks when they are assigned. Every lesson, for example, can introduce or reinforce certain productive mental habits. Similarly, teachers can select and teach key knowledge and skills in introductory lessons that will prepare students for success in completing a meaningful-use task that is presented later on.

An effective clinical supervisor or cognitive/peer coach can use the pre-observation conference to determine with the teacher how a particular lesson may relate to students' preparation for future participation in a meaningful-use task that will involve one or more of the meta-processes identified in Dimension 4: decision making, investigation, experimental inquiry, problem solving, and invention. The pre-observation conference is also an ideal setting for the observer and teacher to examine specific elements of meaningful-use task instruction that can become the focus of an observation session or sessions.

In observing a lesson for key elements related to Dimension 4, clinical supervisors and cognitive/peer coaches can acquire data in response to the following questions:

- To what extent does the lesson prepare students to engage successfully in real-world applications of knowledge through participating in meaningful-use tasks?

- To what extent does the meaningful-use task engage students in reality-based roles, activities, and thinking operations?

- How are students introduced to a meaningful-use task?

- How does the teacher provide modeling for successful student participation in a meaningful-use task involving advanced mental operations?

- To what extent are students given options about final products that will evolve from the completion of a meaningful-use task?

- How are students encouraged to use resources beyond the classroom to complete a meaningful-use task?

- How are oral presentations and defenses integrated into the final aspects of a meaningful-use task?
- How successful are students in responding to complex intellectual tasks requiring the use of such meta-skills as decision making, problem solving, investigation, experimental inquiry, and invention?

The "Examples of Observation Feedback" in Figure 5.1 are designed as an entry point for helping observers and teachers identify key elements of the meaningful-use task observation process. The commendations and recommendations included here are intended only as examples or models. Through the use of such techniques as mirroring, collaborative coaching, and expert coaching, observation partners can begin a meaningful dialogue leading to the improvement of a teacher's use of Dimension 4 strategies and principles.

FIGURE 5.1
Dimension 4
Examples of Observation Feedback

Observing for the Effective Integration of Meaningful-Use Tasks into Students' Instructional Experiences

A. Commendations

- Your lesson reflects a clear commitment to helping students apply their knowledge to reality-based situations and tasks. Your use of a long-term, meaningful-use task to structure this unit clearly helped students internalize the declarative and procedural knowledge they were acquiring.

- Students were especially engaged by the design of the meaningful-use task on which they were working. You very effectively reinforced for students the value and relevance of course content by having students respond to a long-term, real-world scenario in which they assumed a role as a "professional" working on extended decision making, problem solving, investigation, experimental inquiry, and invention.

- Your lesson was an excellent reflection of the design principles of the Dimensions of Learning meaningful-use task, including your allowing for student choice of end products and requiring some form of oral presentation/defense.

- Students' ability to respond effectively to an authentic, meaningful-use task reflects the quality of their previous learning experiences, including their evident mastery, extension, and refinement of essential declarative and procedural knowledge.

- You successfully prepared students to engage in the meaningful-use task you assigned by modeling and providing opportunities for student rehearsal of the major thinking processes implicit in the task.

- Your use of visual representations of essential thinking processes reinforced students' ability to complete the meaningful-use task you assigned.

B. Recommendations

- Explore ways to reinforce students' perceptions of the relevance and purpose of the assignments you give them. Instead of isolated or discrete instructional tasks, consider the periodic use of meaningful-use tasks. These tasks should involve students' long-term engagement in broad-based thinking processes, allow for student choice of end product, reflect real-world scenarios and situations, and incorporate some form of culminating presentation or oral defense.

- Students are unlikely to retain much of the declarative and procedural knowledge they are taught if they are not required to extend, refine, and use it meaningfully in tasks that are long-term and related to the world beyond the classroom.

- When engaging students in a meaningful-use task, make certain that they fully understand, and have opportunities to practice, the major thinking processes required to complete the task.

(*continued*)

- Provide students with a model of the steps or components involved in the various thinking processes that underlie the meaningful-use tasks you assign. For example, if students are expected to engage in a long-term decision-making process, they should have acquired proficiency in the use of a coherent decision-making procedure. Consider the use of a decision matrix to assist students in this area.

- Investigation is an important meta-skill that students can use in a variety of contexts and situations. In addition to the traditional use of historical investigation, explore ways to give students experience in the application of *projective investigation* (dealing with a hypothetical event in the future or in the past) and *definitional investigation* (identifying the specific characteristics and evolution of a key concept).

- Modeling the investigation process should include clear identification of the thing being investigated, identification of what is already known about it, identification and explanation of areas of confusion or contradiction, and development and defense of a plausible resolution to this confusion or contradiction.

- Experimental inquiry does not necessarily belong just in a science or mathematics classroom. Your (English/social studies) students might benefit from its use. The process should include observation, deducing theories or rules about observed phenomena, prediction, hypothesis testing or experimentation, and explanation of results.

- Problem-solving strategies and processes should be integrated into all disciplines. Explore ways to present meaningful-use tasks in which your students apply a strategic problem-solving process to the resolution of a current events problem, an historical issue/problem, or a problem involving fictional characters, for example.

- Invention as a major thinking process is essential to all disciplines and subjects. Consider the periodic incorporation of opportunities for students to develop and display their creativity by producing something new that meets a perceived need.

- In planning for a meaningful-use task, you might consider the following questions to guide the design process:

   – What are the "big issues" in this unit or course?
   – How many issues will be considered?
   – Who will initiate and structure the tasks?
   – What types of products will students be asked to create?
   – To what extent will students be given choice as to final product?
   – To what extent will students work in cooperative groups?
   – How will some form of oral presentation or defense be included?

- In evaluating students' performance on a meaningful-use task, consider two essential issues: (1) the completeness of the processes involved, and (2) the effectiveness of students' thinking and accuracy of the information used.

6

Supporting Students' Mastery of a Core Curriculum: Observing Dimension 2

Planning for effective instruction and strategic learning requires that instructors determine how students can best acquire and integrate the essential knowledge of the curriculum they study. Dimensions of Learning emphasizes student mastery of two important types of knowledge—*declarative* (facts, concepts, generalizations, and principles) and *procedural* (skills, processes, procedures, and performance-based competencies). If students are to be successful in acquiring and using productive mental habits and in completing meaningful-use tasks, they will require essential knowledge and skills to assist them in moving toward those ambitious goals.

An instructor can approach the design of a Dimensions of Learning unit plan from a variety of vantage points. One of the most useful strategies is to begin by identifying the two elements we have discussed in the preceding chapters: (1) the mental habits that will be introduced or reinforced throughout the unit, and (2) the meaningful-use task that all activities in the unit will build toward and support. Once this is accomplished, many Dimensions of Learning users backward-map to Dimension 2. By carefully defining the declarative and procedural knowledge to be taught or reinforced during early phases of the unit, teachers can ensure that students experience later success while working independently on the assigned meaningful-use task.

To successfully implement Dimension 2, teachers and administrators need to clearly formulate and align curriculum, instruction, and assessment so that they answer two key curriculum questions: What do we want students *to know* (declarative knowledge), and what do we want students to be able *to do* (procedural knowledge)? Perhaps the single greatest responsibility of curriculum and program developers in a successful learning organization is to ensure that traditional overloaded, coverage-driven curricula are revised to address these issues. An integrated core curriculum with a clearly defined set of Dimension 2 learner outcomes is crucial to the development of effective instruction. To this end, the following questions can guide the process of observing for Dimension 2:

- What should we be able to observe in a learning organization that successfully integrates Dimension 2 into all phases of its curriculum, instruction, and assessment?

- What can we observe students knowing and doing in a school setting or classroom in which staff successfully articulate and teach for student mastery of essential declarative and procedural knowledge?

- How can clinical supervisors, cognitive and peer coaches, and action research teams support teachers' ability to help students acquire and integrate essential knowledge?

This chapter explores the implications of Dimension 2 for all facets of the observation process. It begins with an overview of how a successful learning organization can assess its implementation of Dimension 2. For example, what should we be able to observe in a school or school system in which declarative and procedural knowledge have been clearly identified? What changes in curriculum, instructional design, and assessment should be evident? The chapter then identifies specific learner behaviors that should be apparent if students are successfully acquiring and integrating declarative and procedural knowledge. Next is a detailed set of options for action research teams to use in examining critical aspects of Dimension 2 implementation. The chapter concludes with suggestions for integrating Dimension 2 into the formal teacher observation process, including ways in which clinical supervisors and cognitive/peer coaches can work with teachers to improve student performance in this area.

Dimension 2 and the Learning Organization

Fundamental to improving an organization's implementation of Dimension 2 is a review of the organization's philosophy of learning. The Dimensions of Learning program reflects recent breakthroughs in learning theory and cognitive research. At its core is the recognition that learning is a constructed process, not an activity in which students passively internalize predigested or preformed knowledge.

As Wiggins (1991) and Sizer (1992) remind us, students are at the heart of that process: they are workers whose workplace is the classroom. Since new learning is shaped by each learner's *prior knowledge*, good instruction dignifies and draws upon that knowledge. Much learning also occurs through *social interaction*, which requires that effective instruction acknowledge the social and cultural nature of the learning process.

Learning is also closely tied to particular situations. The "situated" nature of the process suggests that transfer of a body of information or a skill does not occur easily or automatically. Therefore, teachers must plan for transfer in every lesson and unit. Successful learning involves students' use of numerous strategies, each of which can be taught and reinforced. Ideally, students are helped to incorporate these strategies into a personal repertoire of learning skills that can become a foundation for lifelong learning. Finally, wherever possible, learning events should be experience-based and related to the world beyond the classroom.

Based on the idea that learning is a constructed process, the following questions are designed as a guide for members of the learning organization to review their current programs and plan for successful Dimension 2 implementation:

1. How have we articulated our philosophy of learning within our organization? To what extent does our philosophy align with current cognitive research and learning theory?

2. To what extent do we assess and incorporate students' prior knowledge and experiences into the design of our instructional programs?

3. In what areas of our instructional program have we incorporated and emphasized experiential learning opportunities for all students? In what areas do we need to increase this emphasis?

4. To what extent have we encouraged and supported our staff to make their classrooms interactive, including regular use of cooperative learning structures and techniques?

5. How have we provided training in techniques that are consistent with a constructivist classroom? Have we ensured that all of our staff understand and plan for learning activities that are student-centered? Have we prepared teachers to reinforce students' transfer of knowledge to new situations?

6. Have we assisted students in becoming strategic learners? How have we assisted them in learning how to learn?

7. Have we revised our written curriculum to ensure that it

- Clearly spells out essential facts, concepts, generalizations, and principles that all students are expected to know?

- Clearly specifies essential skills, processes, procedures, and standards-based competencies that all students are expected to master?

- Eliminates unnecessary or nonessential declarative and procedural knowledge so that students have sufficient time to participate in independent meaningful-use tasks?

- Is internally consistent, coherent, and integrated, clearly identifying those topics and themes that function as organizing schema?

8. Does our instructional program ensure that all of our students acquire and integrate essential declarative knowledge by consistently using strategies that help them to

- Construct meaning in response to new information they are presented during active, learner-centered tasks and activities?
- Organize knowledge by using physical and pictographic representations, including graphs, charts, and visual organizers?
- Store essential information by using a variety of memory recall devices?

9. Does our instructional program ensure that all of our students acquire and integrate essential procedural knowledge, by consistently using strategies that help them to

- Experience modeling of key skills, processes, and procedures, including techniques such as think-alouds and mental rehearsal?
- Shape their acquisition of new procedural knowledge through regular, varied, and extensive practice opportunities?
- Set up practice schedules to gain speed and accuracy in applying a new skill or process?

10. Have we made sure that our assessment and evaluation programs are aligned with our curriculum so that we can gather and use a variety of data about the ways students acquire and integrate essential declarative and procedural knowledge?

As suggested previously, students cannot respond successfully to the rigors of an independent meaningful-use task unless they have the knowledge and skills required by it. Members of the learning organization, therefore, should make a concerted effort to identify those student behaviors that can be observed if Dimension 2 has been successfully implemented at a school or system level.

Observing Student Behaviors Consistent with Effective Implementation of Dimension 2

Once again, let us return to our vision of a fully "dimensionized" school environment. What should we be able to observe in students' behavior if they are successfully acquiring and integrating the essential knowledge and skills of their core curriculum? In this facet of the observation process, members of the learning organization might consider the following questions:

1. In acquiring and integrating their knowledge of important declarative elements of the curriculum, can students demonstrate understanding of

- Key characteristics of persons, places, things, and events?
- Key consequences of events?
- Key causal networks and processes?
- Key problems and their solutions?
- Key generalizations and related examples?
- Key examples and defining characteristics of significant concepts?

2. In acquiring and integrating their knowledge of important procedural elements of the curriculum, can students demonstrate important skills and processes

- Without error or with an acceptable amount of error?
- Quickly enough to use them effectively?
- Easily enough to use them effectively?
- In a variety of appropriate settings?

3. Can we observe *all* students actively engaged in the process of acquiring and integrating essential declarative knowledge by

- Constructing meaning through active, learner-centered activities that include cooperative learning, teamwork, reciprocal teaching, and concept attainment exercises?
- Organize new knowledge by creating original physical and pictographic representations, including graphs, charts, and visual organizers?
- Store essential knowledge using a repertoire of memory aids, including such techniques as link strategies and symbol/ substitution techniques?

4. Can we observe all students actively engaged in the process of acquiring and integrating essential procedural knowledge by

- Participating successfully in modeling experiences such as the creation of flow charts, mental rehearsals, and think-aloud exercises?
- Shaping their ability to use a new skill or process through extensive practice opportunities? These might include giving students frequent chances to point out common errors and pitfalls, as well as frequent opportunities to use the skill or process in a variety of situations and settings.

- Internalizing the procedural knowledge by setting up and following practice schedules tied to identified performance standards?

5. Can we acquire student performance data from a variety of sources so that we get as complete a picture as possible of how successfully all students are mastering essential declarative and procedural knowledge?

6. Do we have evidence that all students can transfer essential declarative and procedural knowledge to the successful completion of independent meaningful-use tasks?

7. Can we observe all students acquiring and integrating the knowledge and skills they need to develop such productive habits of mind as self-regulated, critical, and creative thinking?

Students' acquisition and integration of essential knowledge and skills is the heart and soul of an effective assessment process. Dimension 2 therefore represents a rich and fertile ground for identifying potential action research projects that can be used to improve student performance in the learning organization.

The Action Research Process and Dimension 2

Improving student performance is the focus of the action research process. But what knowledge and skills do we want students to acquire and integrate? How do we incorporate key elements of Dimension 2 into curriculum, instruction, and assessment? Perhaps most importantly, how do we plan for equity, ensuring that *all* learners master the necessary knowledge and skills? The following preliminary questions can help guide a school-based or systemwide action research team in investigating these issues:

1. How successfully does our written curriculum reflect the design principles of Dimension 2? For example, how successfully have we identified a core body of declarative and procedural knowledge that all students are expected to master?

2. How successfully have we trained our staff in the use of Dimension 2 techniques and strategies? What evidence can we obtain to confirm our assessment of the extent and quality of Dimension 2 implementation?

3. What problems or issues are affecting students' ability to acquire and integrate essential declarative and procedural knowledge?

4. What data can we gather to confirm that our students can apply essential declarative and procedural knowledge to the successful completion of independent study projects and meaningful-use tasks?

5. As part of our assessment program, how are we collecting and analyzing both formative and summative data related to student progress in the following areas:

- Constructing meaning in response to essential declarative knowledge?

- Organizing essential declarative knowledge?

- Storing essential declarative knowledge?

- Constructing models for acquiring and integrating essential procedural knowledge?

- Shaping essential procedural knowledge?

- Internalizing essential procedural knowledge so that students can use key skills and processes automatically?

6. What does our analysis of disaggregated data reveal about the progress of our students at all grade levels in attaining mastery of essential declarative and procedural outcomes?

7. How can we expand our assessment repertoire to capture the full range of student experiences and progress in mastering essential declarative and procedural knowledge? For example, have we made effective use of portfolio assessment to reflect students' thinking, as well as the breadth of their independent activities while acquiring and integrating new knowledge?

8. To what extent can we say that we have clearly and fully articulated performance standards related to essential declarative and procedural outcomes? To what extent do we have data to confirm that all students are achieving satisfactory progress in attaining these standards?

9. To what extent can we confirm that all students work in an educational environment that continually reflects key Dimension 2 design principles, including regular opportunities to participate in experiential and cooperative learning activities?

In the realm of Dimension 2 implementation, action research offers a particularly useful process for addressing key operational issues. It provides an ideal context for sound decision making. Given the Dimension 2 emphasis on the need for a core curriculum with clearly specified declarative and procedural outcomes and standards, action research can ensure that members of the learning organization make their decisions based on concrete data. The process can also enable research teams to identify key problems and discover practical solutions through the process of shared inquiry. Using Calhoun and Glickman's (1993) five-phase model of action research, staffs might approach the action process by considering these key elements:

1. Selecting a Focus. What is the specific area of student learning in which we are particularly interested? In approaching Dimension 2, we will confront some of the most comprehensive and sweeping aspects of our curriculum and instructional program. How can we narrow our investigation so that it becomes both manageable and practical? Are we most concerned about our students' achievement of designated standards related to their acquisition and use of essential declarative or procedural knowledge? Is it possible that we should combine our approach to concentrate on a fusion of key elements from both domains? Should we select a schoolwide focus, or should we emphasize key components or structural elements of our program, such as student performance in a particular subject or grade level?

2. Collecting Data. Once we have selected our focus for this research project, what objective data do we have available? What does current professional literature tell us about how to improve student performance in the focus area(s) we have identified? To what extent do the sources of data we have available provide a complete and accurate picture of how our students are performing in the area(s) we have selected? To what extent should we expand the repertoire of assessment strategies and approaches we use to monitor student progress in relationship to the declarative and/or procedural standards and outcomes we are investigating?

After a preliminary review of the available data, do we begin to see patterns of student strength and need? For example, is there an overall or aggregate pattern of need related to all students' acquisition and integration of essential facts, concepts, generalizations, and principles? Or do we find specific weaknesses in student performance in certain aspects of our curriculum or among certain subgroups of our overall population?

3. Organizing Data. After we have collected our data, how can we arrange the information so that it is comprehensible to us and to audiences beyond our research team? Have we made sure that we have acquired both quantitative and qualitative data as a basis for our decision-making process? In the case of declarative and procedural knowledge acquisition, how do we make certain that we present an integrated, holistic picture? How do we avoid approaching student learning of essential knowledge and skills as discrete and unrelated elements? How do we emphasize the relationship between the skills and knowledge in our research focus area to students' ability to engage in meaningful-use tasks and develop productive habits of mind?

4. Analyzing and Interpreting Data. How can we best turn the data we have acquired and organized into diagnostic information? How can we integrate supporting information from professional literature into our analysis and interpretation process? In addressing a critical aspect of Dimension 2 implementation, to what extent do our data begin to suggest changes needed in key aspects of our instructional program, such as curriculum design, staff development, scheduling and staffing configurations, and assessment? Once again, how do we present a holistic, integrated picture of Dimension 2 student performance in relationship to the more challenging and complex activities and outcomes associated with dimensions 4 and 5?

5. Taking Action. What can we conclude about our students' performance and needs in relation to our original research focus? What innovations and initiatives should we recommend that we undertake as a group? What innovations and initiatives would we recommend that our entire school or school system consider? Can we now present an action plan that will strategically describe for our staff how we propose to improve students' performance on standards identified for the declarative and procedural knowledge that was the focus of our research? As we conclude our initial action research process, what would we recommend as our

- Primary goals and objectives for improving student performance?
- Key tasks related to achieving these outcomes?
- Target dates for completing each task?
- Designated responsibilities and duties?
- Required resources?
- Key milestones or benchmarks for monitoring the progress of our plan's implementation?
- Formative and summative evaluation strategies?

It is important to keep in mind that the improvement of student performance is dependent on the improvement of teacher performance. The distinctions between strategies for declarative and procedural knowledge should be understood and used by effective instructors. The strategy-specific nature of Dimension 2 makes it a fertile ground for empirical observation and inquiry. The teacher observation process, from the more formal aspects of clinical supervision to the more informal aspects of peer mirroring and collaboration, can strengthen the ability of a learning organization to ensure that all students acquire and integrate core Dimension 2 knowledge and skills.

Dimension 2 and the Teacher Observation Process

In observing for Dimension 2, the coach or observer is acquiring data that answer the following questions:

- What are the specifics of the declarative knowledge that makes up the instructional lesson? Are they appropriate, accurate, complete, and clearly articulated to students?

- How does the instructor present this information to students? Do they experience it directly or indirectly?
- How does the instructor help students construct meaning in relation to the essential declarative knowledge of the lesson?
- How does the instructor help students organize the information presented?
- How does the instructor help students store essential information?
- What skills, processes, and procedures are taught or reinforced during the lesson?
- How does the instructor aid students in constructing models of essential procedural knowledge?
- How does the instructor help students shape skills, processes, and other forms of procedural knowledge?
- How does the instructor help students internalize essential procedural knowledge?
- How does the instructor monitor student acquisition and integration of the declarative and procedural knowledge presented during the lesson?
- How successful are students in mastering the essential declarative and procedural knowledge that make up the core curriculum?

Any one of these questions can become the basis for clinical observation, cognitive coaching, or peer coaching. The "Examples of Observation Feedback" in Figure 6.1 can be used to identify the kinds of instructional elements that can become the focus of a specific observation session. A clinical supervisor or administrative cognitive coach, for example, might explore with the teacher which of the elements he or she might benefit from receiving constructive and expert feedback about during a teaching episode. Similarly, peer coaches can jointly determine which of the key instructional elements they will investigate together. They can agree in advance which of the three peer coaching processes will be employed during a particular session: mirroring, collaborative coaching, or expert coaching.

FIGURE 6.1
Dimension 2
Examples of Observation Feedback

I. Helping Students Construct Meaning for Declarative Knowledge

A. Commendations

- You effectively reinforced students' acquisition and integration of knowledge presented in your lecture by periodically stopping and allowing them to process the information presented.

- Throughout the lesson you encouraged students to use a variety of senses to experience and reinforce their knowledge of essential facts, concepts, generalizations, and principles.

- Through the use of the KWL (Know/Want to Know/Learned) technique at the beginning and end of the lesson, you helped your students construct meaning for essential declarative knowledge.

- You are to be commended for making your instruction as student-centered and as interactive as possible. For example, your use of the concept attainment process allowed students to achieve understanding of key concepts through shared inductive inquiry, rather than through passively listening to a lecture.

- You effectively reinforced student ownership of the lesson material through a consistent use of reciprocal teaching techniques, including the use of dyads, triads, and full-group discussion to summarize, question, clarify, and predict.

- You energized students' responses to key reading selections through a highly interactive and effective Before-During-After approach to reading.

B. Recommendations

- Work on vitalizing your lectures by making them more interactive. Consider, for example, the use of a three-minute pause every 10–15 minutes, in which students individually or in pairs summarize material, identify interesting aspects, and identify areas of confusion or questions they would like clarified.

- The more senses students use when they first experience new information, the greater the likelihood they will learn and retain that knowledge. Please make a greater effort to integrate sensory experiences and activities into the presentation of new information.

- Strive to make your classroom more interactive and student centered through the use of a KWL strategy: at the beginning of a lesson, all students declare what they think they already know about the topic and what they want to know about it; at the end of the lesson, they describe what they learned.

- When introducing students to an important new concept, consider the use of a more inductive or inquiry-based approach. The concept attainment process, for example, provides students initial examples and nonexamples of the concept being taught. As students begin to feel that they understand the concept, they are asked to give their own examples and nonexamples. At the conclusion of the process, the group identifies the correct label for the concept and works with the instructor to identify its major attributes.

- When students are experiencing information through reading, you might vary your instruction by the periodic use of reciprocal teaching. With your guidance, students assume the role of student leaders, then summarize the reading material, pose relevant questions, clarify confusing points, and make predictions about what will happen in the next section of the text to be read.

(*continued*)

- Another effective process for making reading more experience-based and interactive is the Before-During-After strategy. Before reading, students identify what they know about the subject and pose questions and predictions about the passage. During reading, students generate mental pictures, summarize, try to answer previously generated questions, and test predictions made. After reading, students summarize what they have learned and state how they can use that information.

II. Helping Students Organize Declarative Knowledge

A. Commendations

- You made a concerted and positive effort throughout the lesson to help students mentally organize the information they were learning.

- You successfully recognized and attended to students' need to construct meaning and individually organize their understanding of what they are learning.

- You emphasized throughout the lesson that students must organize their acquisition and integration of essential declarative knowledge through processes such as summarizing, outlining, paraphrasing, and using both physical and pictographic representations.

- Students clearly benefited from having to create physical and pictographic representations of the information they were learning during the lesson.

- Your integration into the lesson of student-generated graphs and charts helped your students understand and mentally organize their comprehension of essential quantitative information.

- Your use of graphic organizers at key points in the lesson reinforced for your students the need to develop a personal understanding of organizational patterns through self-generated graphic representations.

- You provided strong guidance to students in organizing information through your presentation of organizer questions prior to students' being taught significant new information.

- You enhanced your students' ability to take notes on key information through your suggestion that they make graphic representations of key declarative knowledge and related patterns.

B. Recommendations

- Students benefit from assistance designed to help them organize the information they are learning; as new information is presented, please work with students to use techniques and strategies that connect prior learning and experience to new declarative knowledge.

- As the knowledge within a lesson or unit becomes increasingly complex, please help students organize their understanding of it through the use of such techniques as summarizing, outlining, paraphrasing, and related organizing strategies.

- Using flow charts, advance organizers, and other forms of graphic representations can be an invaluable way to reinforce students' ability to organize their knowledge and construct meaning in response to new information and skills.

- Essential questions and advance organizer questions are important tools that can help guide and inform student learning; to help students organize new knowledge and relate it to prior knowledge schema, consider incorporating these elements into your repertoire of questioning strategies.

- Pictographs can help students identity and retain key facts, concepts, generalizations, and principles presented in a lesson or unit; please consider using this strategy when you are reviewing key declarative knowledge in a lesson or unit.

(*continued*)

- Several of your students appeared to be experiencing difficulty in organizing and making sense of the information they were studying; consider expanding your use of techniques proven effective in helping students organize essential declarative knowledge, including advance organizer questions, flow charts, advance organizers, and graphic representations of key information.

III. Helping Students Store Declarative Knowledge

A. Commendations

- You did a highly effective job of stressing to students that memorizing essential information is an important and active, rather than passive, process.

- You demonstrated and asked students to use a variety of highly creative memory recall devices to help them remember key information you presented.

- You did a very good job of emphasizing that students must work at storing and retaining essential declarative knowledge, recognizing that these processes do not occur automatically or effortlessly for most people.

- Students benefited immensely from the rich variety of memory aids you asked them to use, including imagining mental pictures of the information, and noticing physical sensations and emotions associated with the information.

- I was very impressed that you asked students to generate and share with others their own ideas for memory devices; having students share their strategies and coach one another in their use was particularly effective.

B. Recommendations

- Many of your students seemed to have trouble retaining essential information from previous lessons. You might consider working with them directly in using a variety of memory aids and devices.

- Model for students those memory strategies proven by research to be effective in helping to store essential declarative knowledge; that is, imagining a mental picture of the information, and noticing physical sensations and emotions associated with the information.

- Students can store important information in long-term memory by translating that information into symbols and substitutes, such as a word that sounds like the information they want to remember and is easy to picture.

- When memorizing sequential or ordered information, students might find the link strategy useful, where they link one image to another in some kind of chain or story, usually a highly creative and even nonsensical one.

- You might consider presenting students with formal systems for storing information, and modeling the use of those systems through extended coaching. Some popular systems you could use include the "rhyming pegword method," the number/picture system, and the "familiar place system." Each of these is described in the *Dimensions of Learning Teacher's Manual.*

- Students might benefit from your encouragement to develop and share their own memory aids and devices; particularly successful aids might be used by other students as they work to store essential declarative knowledge from a lesson or unit.

(continued)

IV. Helping Students Construct Models for Procedural Knowledge

A. Commendations

- When you introduced a new skill to your students, you consistently modeled its use.
- You did a highly commendable job of using think-aloud modeling for your students; the use of "I-statements" reinforced your role as a fellow learner and modeled effective thinking.
- Your students benefited from the clear, well-delineated, written set of steps you presented when introducing procedural knowledge.
- The flow charts you used seemed especially useful in helping students to construct models for the skills and processes they were learning and reinforcing during the lesson.
- I was particularly impressed by your emphasis on metacognition and comprehension monitoring among your students. Your use of mental rehearsals of key skills, for example, reinforced for students the value of this process.

B. Recommendations

- Simply telling students that they must use a specific skill or process often isn't effective. Please place greater emphasis on modeling skills for your students when you present them for the first time.
- Without an initial model, learning a skill or process can be chaotic and time-consuming because it becomes essentially a trial-and-error process. Your students seemed to be experiencing some difficulty mastering the skill you presented because of an absence of modeling.
- When you are introducing a new skill or process, consider using a think-aloud process in which you verbalize your thoughts as you demonstrate that procedural knowledge.
- In order to accommodate students' learning style preferences, you might supplement your modeling of a skill or process by presenting students with a written set of steps.
- The use of a flow chart, particularly if it is student-generated, can be a powerful way of reinforcing a key skill or process. Consider having students create a visual representation of how steps in a process interact, particularly in a lesson in which students have been initially exposed to that procedural knowledge.
- Mental rehearsal can help reinforce students' acquisition of a basic model of an essential skill or process. Encourage students to review the steps of a process in their mind without actually performing them.

V. Helping Students Shape Procedural Knowledge

A. Commendations

- Your lesson reflected positive, careful attention to the need to demonstrate and provide practice for students in the important variations of essential skills and processes.
- You reinforced very effectively students' acquisition and integration of key skills by your demonstration of common errors and pitfalls, as well as by coaching students when their behavior reflected errors and pitfalls.
- All students appeared to benefit from your emphasis on the use of key skills in a variety of situations and contexts, including examples generated by the students themselves.

(continued)

B. Recommendations

- Your students would benefit from more extensive opportunities to shape and refine the essential skills they are learning. Inattention to shaping a new skill is a primary reason for many students' failure to effectively use basic skills and processes.

- If you do not give students opportunities to practice variations of a skill or process, they will not be able to apply that skill or process in a new or unique context. They remain dependent on the formula they were initially taught, with no freedom to vary from the formula.

- Consider the use of coaching, by yourself as well as by other students, to help students learn how to avoid common errors and pitfalls when using a skill or process.

- You gave students little opportunity to shape the procedural knowledge they were learning; please provide them with a greater variety of situations in which to use a specific skill or process.

VI. Helping Students Internalize Procedural Knowledge

A. Commendations

- Your students appeared to master the essential skills and processes you were teaching them at a clear level of automaticity. It is apparent that they have internalized those skills as a result of extensive rehearsal in a variety of settings and contexts.

- Your lesson was a particularly effective example of the benefits of massed practice; all students were encouraged to practice key skills immediately and frequently.

- Using a practice schedule appeared to pay major dividends; students seemed to be learning essential procedural knowledge at a deep level and were able to retrieve it automatically.

- Students appeared to develop fluency in the use of key skills and processes as a result of your encouraging them to chart their accuracy.

- Your requirement that students chart both their accuracy and their speed while rehearsing essential skills and processes effectively reinforced their development of fluency and automaticity in skill application.

B. Recommendations

- Many of your students appeared to be able to use key skills and processes in only a predictable or formulaic way. Encourage them to use a practice schedule in order to master skill usage at a level of automaticity.

- Consider the use of peer coaching as part of classroom activities designed to reinforce students' ability to apply skills accurately in a variety of settings and situations.

- It is imperative that you give students performance standards and that they evaluate their individual progress in relationship to those standards. You might consider having students chart their accuracy when practicing new skills and processes, particularly in relationship to the standards you have identified.

- If students are to be effective in using essential procedural knowledge, you must give them opportunities to develop fluency in the use of key skills and processes. Have students chart their speed when learning a new skill or process. Also, ask them to continue to compare their performance against the standards you have given them or that the class as a whole has generated.

7

Internalizing the Language of Thinking: Observing Dimension 3

A major problem many students experience is an inability to apply the declarative and procedural knowledge they have learned. In the most effective learning situations, students receive instruction that helps them extend and refine essential facts, concepts, generalizations, principles, skills, and processes. Dimension 3, extending and refining knowledge, encourages teachers to design and implement instructional activities and tasks that require student thinking more rigorous than that needed for the initial acquisition and integration of knowledge.

Specifically, Dimension 3 strategies, activities, and processes are present in the classroom when a teacher (1) directly teaches students a specific thinking skill or operation through modeling and student rehearsal, (2) reinforces students' ability to articulate the basic components of that skill or operation, and (3) provides a variety of opportunities for students to use that skill or operation. In exploring the Dimension 3 implementation process, school-based and systemwide teams confront the following key questions:

- How successfully have we defined and communicated the mental operations needed by students to extend and refine their use of essential declarative and procedural knowledge?

- How do we help our students develop their knowledge and skills in new and unusual ways that exceed their original understanding?

- How do we make sure that the direct teaching of key thinking operations becomes a vital part of our curriculum, instruction, and assessment processes?

This chapter begins by examining how Dimension 3 might manifest itself in an effective learning organization. What kinds of behavior, for example, should we be able to observe in administrators, supervisors, and instructional staff if extending and refining processes function well at a school site or in a school system? Next, the chapter explores what we can observe if students are successful in extending and refining their content knowledge.

It then suggests how an action research team might identify and investigate key issues and problems that affect student learning of Dimension 3 skills and behaviors. Finally, the chapter explores in detail how Dimension 3 behaviors can become the focus of the teacher observation process.

Dimension 3 and the Learning Organization

The school or school system successfully implementing Dimension 3 has developed and implemented a core curriculum that clearly defines how students acquire and integrate thinking skills and operations throughout their K–12 experience. Essential thinking processes should form a crucial and explicit part of every lesson, unit, and curriculum guide. Instruction at all levels and in all disciplines should reinforce students' ability to extend and refine essential declarative and procedural knowledge. Similarly, assessments should emphasize instruments that allow for more than pick-the-right-answer testing. Performance assessment strategies, including portfolio assessments, should make up a significant part of a learning organization's approach to monitoring student progress.

In observing and assessing itself as a learning organization, a school or school system might consider the following key questions as a starting point:

1. To what extent does our written curriculum clearly and explicitly identify essential thinking skills and mental operations that we expect all students to master throughout their K–12 educational experience? How have we identified specific thinking skills that are particularly important for student mastery within each discipline or program that makes up our core curriculum? How have we reinforced the integration of essential thinking skills across disciplines and programs? In what ways does our curriculum ensure that essential extending and refining skills contribute to students' ability to successfully complete long-term, meaningful-use tasks ?

2. To what extent does our written curriculum indicate how students will be introduced to, practice, and reinforce the following thinking operations:

- *Comparison*: identifying and articulating similarities and differences between things?

- *Classifying*: grouping things into definable categories on the basis of their attributes?

- *Induction*: inferring unknown generalizations or principles from observation or analysis?

- *Deduction*: inferring unstated consequences and conditions from given principles and generalizations?

- *Error analysis*: identifying and articulating errors in their thinking or in that of others?
- *Constructing support*: building a system of support or proof for an assertion?
- *Abstracting*: identifying and articulating the underlying theme or general pattern of information?
- *Analyzing perspectives*: identifying and articulating their personal perspectives, as well as the perspectives of others?

3. How successfully have we trained teachers to teach thinking skills and operations directly, as part of their classroom unit and lesson design and delivery?

4. How successfully have we institutionalized a unit plan format and related lesson plan format that reinforce students' ability to extend and refine their use of essential declarative and procedural knowledge?

5. To what extent does our formal teacher observation process encourage and support instructional use of extending and refining techniques and strategies?

6. How have we made certain that our assessment process generates meaningful longitudinal data concerning students' progress in mastering Dimension 3 outcomes?

7. As a staff, how successfully do we practice the application of Dimension 3 thinking skills and operations on a daily basis?

8. How successfully have we provided opportunities for our parents and community members to learn how to reinforce key elements of Dimension 3 learning behaviors?

9. To what extent do we celebrate and acknowledge students' successful use of extending and refining skills and operations?

10. How have we made certain that Dimension 3 activities and outcomes complement all phases of a successful instructional process, rather than becoming artificial add-ons?

In a school or school system that has successfully implemented Dimension 3, we should be able to collect tangible evidence by observing transformed student actions and performance. The following section provides a detailed profile of how to observe for student behavior patterns consistent with mastery of essential extending and refining skills and processes.

Observing Student Behaviors Consistent with Effective Implementation of Dimension 3

Not only should students be taught to use key thinking skills successfully, they should also be able to apply the language of thinking in a conscious and strategic way. Of particular significance is students' ability to internalize the language of thinking. To begin their assessment of Dimension 3 implementation, members of a learning organization might wish to consider one or more of the following questions that address these concerns:

1. How completely, accurately, and effectively is the individual student able to

- Identify specific elements to be *compared*, state the essential characteristics on which they are to be compared, and state clearly the extent to which each element possesses each characteristic?

- Identify specific elements to be *classified*, identify categories into which they will be classified, and assess the extent to which each element fits into those categories?

- Identify specific elements from which to make *inductions*, articulate the reasoning that links each element with the conclusion, and ensure that the conclusions naturally follow from the elements used to draw them?

- Articulate the specific rules or principles from which *deductions* were made, check to determine if the necessary conditions were in place to make the deduction valid, and explain the connection between the articulated rule or principle and the student's conclusions?

- Apply a coherent *error analysis* process, including being able to acknowledge when something was wrong with a body of information or process, specify what was wrong, identify how errors affect it, and describe how errors might be corrected?

- Distinguish between information that requires support and information that does not, offer support for a specific claim, and use a specific method when *constructing support*?

- Clearly identify the main points of literal information, derive from them a coherent *abstract pattern*, and successfully relate that pattern to other information?

- *Analyze perspectives* surrounding a debatable issue or topic, including being able to express an opinion about a specific concept or statement, describe the values underlying that opinion, describe the reasoning behind articulated values, describe values opposing those he or she has expressed, and describe reasoning that supports the opposing value?

2. How successfully do students demonstrate their mastery of essential declarative and procedural knowledge while engaged in extending and refining activities?

3. What evidence can we obtain to confirm that *all* students can apply important Dimension 3 thinking skills and operations to the successful completion of meaningful-use tasks?

4. To what extent do *all* students demonstrate the use of productive mental habits while responding to Dimension 3 activities?

The emphasis on the word *all* in these questions reinforces the need to consider the principle of equity in observing for successful Dimension 3 implementation. It is important that school-based and systemwide improvement teams consider this critical component of a successful learning organization as they explore potential action research projects to improve student performance.

The Action Research Process and Dimension 3

Dimension 3 thinking skills and operations should be an integral part of all students' academic and intellectual repertoire. Unfortunately, as Oakes (1985) and other researchers have confirmed, the tendency for schools in the United States to sort and select students through tracking and ability grouping has produced the phenomenon of cognitive have's and have not's. Until recently, the direct teaching of thinking skills and mental operations was often reserved for programs serving populations labeled "gifted and talented."

Today, thanks to the work of Gardner (1983) and others, learning organizations are increasingly recognizing that all students have unique gifts and talents that should be nurtured. Providing educational programs that promote excellence for all is a major systemic commitment for the effective learning organization. School-based and systemwide teams working on collaborative research in this area might consider the following process and questions to guide their work:

1. Selecting a Focus. What area of student learning is of particular interest or concern to us as we explore the implementation of Dimension 3? Is there a specific area of the curriculum or overall instructional program in which some or all of our students appear to be having difficulty? Are there particular equity issues we might explore in relationship to key thinking skills and processes? Where in our curriculum have we identified Dimension 3 extending and refining outcomes? How successfully do these thinking skills and operations align with the content students are expected to master? As we begin to narrow our focus, how can we justify our decisions concerning the area we wish to investigate? Why is the problem or barrier we have elected to resolve important to us as members of a learning organization? How can we frame our focus in the form of a controlling research question or questions?

2. Collecting Data. What objective information about students in our school or school system relates to our designated focus area and research question(s)? For example, if we are researching how to improve students' ability to use the skills of comparison and classification, what evidence can we obtain about the quality of their aggregate and disaggregated performance in those areas? In addition to standardized test data, do we have other data sources we can use, including student portfolios and performance on meaningful-use tasks?

If the desired information is unavailable or limited, the action research group may need to consider developing instruments to elicit formative and summative data to guide their research process. For example, could the action research team develop some form of observation or assessment protocol for teachers and administrators monitoring student performance in the designated Dimension 3 skills and operations?

The group will also need to consider the scope of its research process, including the time available. For example, are we looking at data related to all of our students, or only selected groups? Are we examining available data from all subjects and grade levels, or are we concentrating our research on specific subjects or age groupings? Finally, are we considering only the current academic year, or do we wish to examine longitudinal data from several school years?

3. Organizing Data. As we complete our initial phase of data collection, we will need to consider how to make our data accessible and comprehensible to all of the key decision makers to whom we will present it. As we sort and categorize the information we have acquired, how can we display it so that we reflect significant patterns, themes, and trends? The action research group will also have to decide how to deal with different forms of quantitative and qualitative data, including the integration of less formal data such as anecdotal reactions and responses from staff and students during interview sessions. Since equity issues may be of paramount concern in this area, the group will need to explore ways to present both aggregate and disaggregated data, categorized under such headings as gender, race, ethnicity, and socio-economic groups.

4. Analyzing and Interpreting Data. As we begin to examine the data, what are the major inferences we can draw about students' learning behaviors and attitudes in the Dimension 3 focus areas we have researched? What does our analysis and interpretation process reveal about the learning environment we have created? To what extent does it appear to reinforce conditions that allow all students to master and apply the Dimension 3 cognitive skills and operations we studied? Do the data suggest that certain subgroups within our student population are doing better—or worse—than a majority of our students? What inferences can we make about modifications needed in our curriculum, instruction, and assessment processes? It is at this point that the action research group may wish to examine the relationship between professional development and student improvement in the focus area. What does the data analysis reveal about key strengths and needs in staff knowledge as related to Dimension 3 strategies and techniques? How can we improve students' use of the skills and operations that were the focus of the research study?

5. Taking Action. As the action research process concludes, the group will need to relate the acquired data and its analysis to the development of a strategic plan that will be presented to decision makers. In particular, how do we propose that student subgroups identified as requiring special intervention receive the support they need to master the outcomes that were the focus of the study? As we conclude our initial action research process, what would we recommend as our

- Essential goals and objectives for improving student performance?
- Key tasks related to achieving these outcomes?
- Target dates for completing each task?
- Designated responsibilities and duties?
- Required resources?
- Key milestones or benchmarks for monitoring the progress of our plan's implementation?
- Formative and summative evaluation strategies?

A powerful way for action research teams to acquire significant data related to Dimension 3 is to examine trends and patterns during teacher observations. For example, what can we observe about teachers' use of important extending and refining techniques and strategies? Most importantly, how can teachers be coached to improve instructional delivery so that all students learn to use Dimension 3 thinking skills and operations?

Dimension 3 and the Teacher Observation Process

In observing for Dimension 3, clinical supervisors and cognitive/peer coaches should work with teachers to acquire data related to the following key questions:

- How does the instructor reinforce essential declarative and procedural knowledge by giving students varied opportunities to extend and refine that knowledge?

- How does the instructor introduce students to a specific thinking skill, process, or operation?
- How does the instructor present students with a general strategy for using the thinking skill, process, or operation?
- How does the instructor present students with different ways to apply the thinking skill, process, or operation?
- How does the instructor help students develop a deep structural understanding of the thinking skill, process, or operation and its essential components?
- How does the instructor help students develop mastery of each of the following thinking processes:

  –Comparison

  –Classification

  –Induction

  –Deduction

  –Error analysis

  –Constructing support

  –Abstraction

  –Analysis of perspectives

- How successfully do students apply the language of thinking to instructional tasks that require the use of complex reasoning skills?

There are a variety of entry points for observing teachers' Dimension 3 behaviors. Pre-observation planning sessions should be used to determine which elements the clinical supervisor or cognitive/peer coach will concentrate on during the observation process. As the "Examples of Observation Feedback" in Figure 7.1 suggest, observation can focus on a teacher's use of questioning strategies, introduction of Dimension 3 concepts, and/or provision of general cognitive strategies for using a particular skill or operation. Dimension 3 observation can also explore how the instructor provides students with ways to graphically represent essential thinking skills and operations. Finally, observers can concentrate on teachers' structuring of skill- and operation-related tasks, as well as their use of student-structured tasks that extend and refine essential knowledge.

The examples in Figure 7.1, like the others in this book, are intended as models and vehicles for discussion. They are means to observation ends, not ends in themselves. By modeling commendations and recommendations after the examples listed here, observers can develop effective feedback for teachers implementing Dimension 3.

FIGURE 7.1
Dimension 3
Examples of Observation Feedback

I. Helping Students Extend and Refine Knowledge Through Questioning

A. Commendations

- Your lesson nicely reinforced the power of effective questioning to strengthen students' ability to extend and refine their knowledge.

- Students benefited from your use of a variety of question types, including knowledge/recall, analytical, evaluative, and interpretive questions.

- You were particularly effective in helping to extend and refine students' knowledge through the use of questions that required thinking processes such as comparison, classification, and error analysis.

- You reinforced students' ability to extend and refine their knowledge by posing thinking-skills-related questions before, during, and after they engaged in learning experiences.

B. Recommendations

- The way you structure and pose questions to students can make a significant difference in how effectively they learn the material you are presenting. Consider varying your question types; you devoted much of your lesson to having students respond to knowledge/recall questions.

- Incorporate question types designed to engage students in critical evaluation and analysis.

- When exploring a piece of writing rich in ideas, you might consider using one or more interpretive questions. These questions have no single correct answer, but they elicit a variety of responses from students and can be supported through the use of textual references as evidence.

- Explore ways to use extending and refining questions that introduce and reinforce students' use of the following mental processes:

  - *Comparison*: How are these things alike? How are they different?

  - *Classification*: Into what groups could you organize these things? What are the rules for membership in each group? What are the defining characteristics of each group?

  - *Induction*: Based on the following facts (observations), what can you conclude? Based on this information, what is a similar conclusion?

  - *Deduction*: Based on the following generalizations (rules, principles), what prediction can you make or what conclusions can you draw that must be true? If you know that _____ has happened, then what do you know will have to occur?

  - *Error analysis*: What are the errors in reasoning in the following information? How is this information misleading?

  - *Constructing support*: What is an argument that would support this claim? What are the limitations or assumptions underlying this argument? How is this information trying to persuade you?

  - *Abstraction*: What is the general pattern underlying this information? To what other situations can this general pattern be applied?

  - *Analysis of perspectives*: Why would someone consider this to be good (bad, neutral)? What is the reasoning behind this perspective? What is an alternative perspective, and what is the reasoning behind it?

(continued)

II. Helping Students Extend and Refine Knowledge Through the Use of Key Thinking Processes

A. Commendations

- Your lesson helped students extend and refine essential declarative and procedural knowledge by requiring them to apply that knowledge using thinking processes such as comparison, abstraction, and analysis of perspectives.

- I was particularly impressed by your attention to the need to directly teach key thinking processes to students.

- Your students clearly benefited from your presentation of key steps in thinking processes such as classification and deduction.

- Just as students benefit from the graphic organizers and flow charts to learn essential declarative knowledge, your students benefited from the use of graphic representations of complex thinking processes such as induction and constructing support.

- Your lesson provided an effective mixture of thinking-skills-based tasks that you designed and that students had a role in designing for themselves.

B. Recommendations

- You expected your students to engage in several tasks requiring the use of key thinking processes for which they clearly lacked knowledge and experience. If a lesson or unit requires that students be able to compare or classify things or ideas, for example, you need to introduce the processes of comparison and classification to students and give them opportunities to reinforce their use of those processes.

- Your students might benefit from a list of steps involved in the use of a particular mental skill or process such as analysis of perspectives.

- When introducing or reinforcing students' understanding and use of mental processes such as error analysis, induction, and deduction, you might consider providing students with a way of graphically representing those processes.

- In addition to tasks you design, you might consider allowing students to design their own approaches to using extending and refining processes.

8

Addressing and Enhancing the Affective Domain: Observing Dimension 1

According to the authors of the *Dimensions of Learning Teacher's Manual* (Marzano et al. 1992a, p. 5), "Learning occurs in a sea of attitudes and perceptions that the effective teacher continually manages—often so skillfully that students are not aware of her efforts. Subtle though this behavior may be, it is a conscious instructional act that involves overtly cultivating specific attitudes and perceptions." No student can be successful in a class if he or she lacks positive attitudes and perceptions about self, peers, the instructor, and the value of the tasks that make up the lesson. Regardless of how ambitious and well-articulated a written curriculum may be, no genuine and lasting learning will occur if students do not perceive themselves as valuable and valued members of the learning community.

Dimension 1 is a bit like the armature of a sculpture or the foundation of a building. In many ways it is invisible but felt as a controlling and defining element; without it, no other components of the learning organization can function successfully. In observing for Dimension 1, therefore, school and system teams must deal with the following key questions:

- How does the school as a learning organization help students feel accepted?

- How does the school help students develop a sense of comfort and order in all areas and aspects of their educational experience?

- How are curriculum and instruction organized to help students perceive tasks as valuable?

- How are students helped to understand and be clear about the tasks they are assigned?

The subtlety and the power of key Dimension 1 elements place this dimension at the heart of an effective learning organization. This chapter begins with a detailed exploration of how Dimension 1 principles and strategies can be observed in a school or school system successfully working to implement them. It then moves to a discussion of what we can observe in learner behaviors when instruction effectively facilitates students' development of positive attitudes and perceptions about themselves, their peers, the instructor, and assigned tasks. The action research component of this chapter offers suggestions for using the five-phase research process to investigate and develop action plans that will solve problems related to organizational and classroom culture and climate issues. Finally, the chapter explores in detail the teacher observation process as it relates to Dimension 1 implementation.

Dimension 1 and the Learning Organization

A school or school system striving to practice Senge's concept of metanoia must look carefully at how it establishes and reinforces a positive and productive institutional culture and climate. Whereas dimensions 2 through 5 explicitly stress students' cognitive, intellectual, and academic development, Dimension 1 emphasizes their growth as feeling, sensing, and social beings. In Dimension 1 we begin to address what Glatthorn (1987a, 1987b), English (1992), and others have called the "organic" and the "hidden" curriculum. What, for example, are the long-range and broadly defined outcomes and behaviors that schools encourage among students and staff members (i.e., the organic curriculum)? What are the unplanned or unconscious outcomes generated by the way a school is organized, governed, or managed, particularly those contradictions between what a school says it values in learner behavior, versus what it actually facilitates in observable student performance (i.e., the hidden curriculum)?

In addressing and enhancing the ways that a school or school system deals with the affective domain of learning, school improvement teams may wish to consider the following questions in observing for Dimension 1:

- How do we ensure that teachers establish productive and supportive relationships with all students in their classes?

- How do we monitor our attitudes about one another, our students, and parents and community members?

- To what extent have we made effective use of strategies, techniques, and programs that enable teachers to engage in equal and positive classroom behaviors that encourage a climate and culture of equity and excellence?

- How successfully have we made use of cooperative learning structures and activities in all of our classrooms?

- To what extent have we created and maintained a safe and orderly environment conducive to all students developing positive attitudes and perceptions about learning?

- To what extent have we made certain that all students and staff clearly understand and "own" our organizational rules, policies, and procedures?

- How have we created a community of learners among our staff and students? How have we made certain that all learners can experience success in our educational environment?

- To what extent have we organized and delivered learning experiences to ensure that students perceive the classroom and the school as a setting that they value and in which they can succeed?

- How successful have our professional development programs and activities been at reinforcing staff use of strategies to help students develop positive attitudes and perceptions about learning?

- How do we monitor, assess, and evaluate the learning climate and organizational culture?

To deal with the breadth and complexity of these issues, school improvement and action research teams might begin by considering which observable student behaviors are generally present in a school environment that has successfully implemented Dimension 1.

Observing Student Behaviors Consistent with Effective Implementation of Dimension 1

Whereas cognitive or intellectual behaviors are relatively accessible for observation and assessment purposes, collecting data related to students' affective or internal responses and reactions is often a more challenging process. This is especially true if school improvement teams are looking for objective evidence rather than snap judgments and seat-of-the-pants anecdotes. In observing for Dimension 1, individuals and groups might consider the following questions as guides to assessing student performance:

- What evidence can we obtain to confirm that students feel connected to their teachers in a positive and productive way?

- To what extent do all students in our school appear to volunteer their opinions?

- How do our students respond when they give incorrect or incomplete responses? What evidence do we have that they feel encouraged to be active participants in their classes?

- When students are participating in cooperative learning activities, to what extent do they understand designated roles and responsibilities? To what extent do they assume responsibility both as an individual and as part of their learning group?
- To what extent do all students demonstrate their ability to use strategies for gaining acceptance from peers and teachers?
- How frequently do our students participate in activities that involve physical movement?
- What evidence do we have that all students appear to understand and "own" classroom rules and procedures?
- Based on direct observation and student feedback, to what extent do our students experience our school as a safe, orderly, and supportive learning environment?
- What evidence do we have that students experience a direct relationship between personal interests, experiences, goals, and the learning activities in which they engage?
- To what extent do all students express clarity and understanding about the instructional tasks they are assigned? To what extent do all students express enthusiasm and assurance that they can be successful in completing the tasks they are given?

Observing Dimension 1 student behaviors can involve the use a variety of processes and instruments. In addition to direct observations as a basis for data collection, school improvement and action research team members may wish to consider other approaches, including

- One-to-one interviews
- Small-group interviews
- Student focus groups
- Parent and community focus group research
- Portfolio content analysis
- School and system climate survey instruments
- Self-assessment evaluation questionnaires
- Staff compilations of personal reflections and anecdotal data
- Videotaped and audiotaped student reflections.

The Action Research Process and Dimension 1

Using a wide variety of data sources to monitor students' attitudes and perceptions about learning is an invaluable component of an action research process related to implementing Dimension 1. Using the student observation questions on pages 88–89 as a starting point, school-based action research teams may wish to consider the following issues as part of their work:

1. Selecting a Focus. Are there major problems or issues in our school culture and climate about which we are especially concerned? As we explore these institutional barriers, what are our collective and individual perceptions about how these problems are affecting students' self-image, social interactions, and academic performance? To what extent are the problems we identify associated with key elements of Dimension 1—that is, a failure to help all students feel accepted, insufficient support for students to develop a sense of comfort and order, and/or inconsistent help for students to perceive tasks as valuable and to understand clearly what we expect of them?

As we explore these issues, can we identify specific problems in our organizational culture and climate to help us narrow down and provide a controlling focus for our investigation?

Dimension 1 action research should always take into consideration key equity issues. Even if a majority of students are not experiencing problems, there may be significant groups or subgroups that require careful attention.

2. Collecting Data. While Dimension 1 elements are among the most important aspects of an effective learning organization, they are also among the most subtle and difficult for which to acquire concrete, objective data that will guide and inform the action research process. Therefore, the data collection phase must be approached with great care and commitment. Professional literature is a good starting point. Similarly, the background research that underlies such programs as TESA (Teacher Expectations and Student Achievement) and GESA (Gender and Ethnic Expectations Student Achievement) can provide an excellent complement to available Dimension 1 materials and resources.

If the action research team is experiencing difficulty in narrowing its focus to one or two key climate issues, they may wish to administer an organizational climate survey to staff, students, and parents. Or they may wish to use the Teacher and Student Self-Assessment Forms in the *Dimensions of Learning Teacher's Manual* (Marzano et al. 1992a, pp. 27–28) to collect data. Other qualitative research instruments can also be used here, including formal and informal interviews, other forms of survey research, and focus group discussion of perceived climate and culture issues and problems. Also, disaggregation of data according to categories such as race, ethnicity, and gender can provide invaluable insights.

3. Organizing Data. Given the affective emphasis of Dimension 1, sorting and categorizing data information becomes another significant aspect of the action research process. Once team members have accessed and elicited sufficient data from a variety of sources and instruments, they must explore how to make the data meaningful and objective to everyone involved in the decision-making process. What, for example, can we infer from such data sources as interviews, videotaped and audiotaped reaction sessions, focus group data, and open-ended survey questionnaires? How do we discern themes, motifs, patterns, and trends evident in the narratives we generate through these instruments and data collection methods? How do we ensure an effective balance between our action research team's abstractions and conclusions, and the concrete material from which they are derived? There is also the critical issue of confidentiality, particularly in our use of videotapes and audiotapes as evidence to confirm our inferences. How can we make sure we do not compromise anyone's privacy, while maintaining our ability to use data sources to support our conclusions?

4. Analyzing and Interpreting Data. In research issues related to organizational culture and climate, the tendency to use qualitative data sources, particularly research narratives, requires careful group analysis and interpretation of themes, patterns, trends, and narrative schema. What will be the group's approach to analyzing interview data? What kind of analytical protocol will the group apply to reflections, open-ended questionnaire responses, and other forms of participant recollection? How will the group ensure that particularly powerful or emotional narratives do not skew the analysis and interpretation of the overall available data?

During this phase of the action research process, the group needs to pay particular attention to aggregated versus disaggregated data trends. For example, is there evidence that students representing certain programs, racial or ethnic groups, or socioeconomic categories reflect collective experiences that are not represented in the overall student population? Is there evidence of a gender division related to the focus area we have selected?

Finally, the research team needs to decide how it will present its data, conclusions, and recommendations to the decision-making individuals and groups that make up its intended audience.

5. Taking Action. At this phase of the process, the group must decide on a course of action to improve those aspects of school culture and climate that were the major focus of their study. Based on our data collection, analysis, and interpretation process, what final conclusions and recommendations can we make in response to our original action research question(s)? Which key components of the strategic plan will we share with the rest of the staff to execute the decisions we have made as a result of the process? How will we identify and justify recommendations concerning the following elements of our strategic plan?

- Major goals and objectives
- Recommended strategies
- Relevant activities extending from identified strategies
- Individual(s) and group(s) responsible for identified activities
- Time line/implementation plan
- Milestones/benchmarks: key points in our implementation process that will be used to generate data concerning student and program progress toward achieving specific objectives
- Evaluation plan explicitly tied to identified outcomes
- Management plan

Although any action research process involves long-range, collaborative inquiry and analysis, the sensitive nature of Dimension 1 issues requires that collaboration be evident in all phases of investigation and decision making. The same caveat applies to clinical supervision and cognitive/peer coaching partnerships. In exploring ways to improve students' attitudes and perceptions about themselves as learners, and about their peers, teachers, and assigned tasks, observers must be particularly sensitive to the affective needs and reactions of the teacher with whom they are working. The next section of this chapter explores in detail how the teacher observation process can become a catalyst for improving student performance within the domain of Dimension 1.

Dimension 1 and the Teacher Observation Process

Dimension 1 offers numerous possibilities for focusing both formal and informal teacher observations. In a pre-observation planning session, the observer and teacher can identify and agree to investigate a wide variety of both verbal and nonverbal behaviors that contribute to classroom climate and culture. During the observation process, the clinical supervisor or cognitive/peer coach is acquiring data concerning such questions as the following:

- How does the instructor help students feel accepted?
- How does the instructor help students develop a sense of comfort and order?
- How does the instructor help students perceive assigned tasks as valuable?
- How does the instructor help students believe that they can perform classroom tasks successfully?

- How does the instructor help students understand the tasks they are assigned?
- To what extent do students demonstrate that they feel positive about themselves, their peers, their instructor, and the tasks they are assigned?

In observing a teacher's approach to helping students feel accepted and ensuring they develop a sense of comfort and order, the observer can target several areas for focus. In the nonverbal range, as identified by Costa and Garmston (1994), a clinical supervisor or peer coach might plan to observe for such teacher behaviors as mannerisms, movement throughout the classroom, and nonverbal feedback to students (e.g., body language, eye contact, and proximity). Particularly important is the issue of how the instructor meets diverse student needs, including how well he or she considers and makes allowances for different ability levels, cognitive styles, emotional needs, and cultural differences.

On the verbal level, a teacher may exhibit a variety of behavior patterns that promote acceptance, comfort, and order. Any of these can become the focus of the observation process. How, for example, do the teacher's verbal mannerisms and feedback to students reinforce or negate their self-perception as a valued member of a learning community? How do the instructor's response behaviors (e.g., use of silence, accepting, paraphrasing, empathizing) and patterns of interaction reinforce or contradict a supportive, nurturing classroom environment? Finally, to what extent is there evidence of an equitable distribution of teacher responses?

A clinical supervisor or cognitive/peer coach can provide valuable insights to a teacher regarding subtle and not-so-subtle behaviors that show how he or she distributes responses. For example, is there a pattern of the teacher favoring one gender over the other, or responding more frequently to students who demonstrate greater language proficiency or perceived ability in the content being taught? Does a student's physical location in the room contribute to his or her ability to become an active and acknowledged member of the classroom learning community?

Both verbal and nonverbal behavior patterns can contribute significantly to students' self-perceptions and their perceptions of tasks as valuable and manageable. At the nonverbal level, for example, the observer might agree to collect data about the instructor's use of time, including his or her handling of interruptions, transitions, punctuality, and interactions with both individual students and groups. Lesson pacing can become another significant observation focus. The observer might examine such behaviors as the instructor's tempo and rhythm, coverage of identified declarative and procedural knowledge, and control of each segment of the lesson. Another focus might be the issue of learning modalities, including how the teacher balances visual, kinesthetic, and auditory modes of instruction.

At the verbal level, the observation process might target the teacher's specific approaches to designing and delivering a lesson that all students understand and at which they can all be successful. How, for example, does the teacher communicate to students the desired outcomes of the lesson and reinforce their understanding of how they are individually and collectively moving toward achieving those objectives? Similarly, how clear is the teacher's overall presentation? This focus area might explore the extent to which the teacher's directions, assignments, modeling, and checking for understanding contribute to student mastery of identified performance targets. Within this domain, the observer and teacher might agree to examine the effectiveness of specific activities and teaching strategies. For example, how successful were processes such as lectures, group activities, lab exercises, discussions, and use of educational technologies to reinforce productive student learning?

The "Examples of Observation Feedback" in Figure 8.1 may help guide and inform an observation session or process that involves a teacher's use of Dimension 1 principles and strategies. As suggested throughout this book, these examples are designed as representative samples only. They are not intended to be complete in themselves. Instead, they can be- come discussion points as the observer and teacher collaborate on improving students' attitudes and perceptions about the learning process.

FIGURE 8.1

Dimension 1
Examples of Observation Feedback

I. Helping Students Feel Accepted

A. Commendations

- Throughout the lesson, you made a conscious and effective effort to reinforce a positive relationship with every student in the class.

- You appeared to have high expectations for all your students, interacting with them in such a way that you reinforced their ability to succeed in the tasks you assigned.

- Through eye contact, movement, and acknowledgment of student input, you continually engaged in equal and positive classroom behaviors throughout the lesson.

- When students gave incorrect or insufficient responses, you effectively made use of such techniques as dignifying their input, restating your questions, and providing hints and cues.

- You reinforced students' feelings of acceptance by their peers through the continual integration of cooperative learning activities and structures into your lesson.

- Through an emphasis on positive qualities and behaviors, you provided students with input and strategies for gaining acceptance from their peers.

B. Recommendations

- Try to establish a more positive relationship with all students in your class through such small but important actions as greeting students at the door as they enter class, using students' names more frequently, and integrating students' interests into discussions.

- When you interact with students, try to consciously keep in mind positive expectations about their behavior in your classroom.

- Make certain that you attend to all quadrants of the room; freely move about all sections of the room.

- Try to establish contact with every student in your classroom.

- Consider rearranging your classroom furniture to allow you clear and easy access to all students and them to you.

- Attribute ownership of ideas to the students who initiated them.

- When students give wrong answers or no response, you might use one or more of the following techniques: give credit to the aspects of an incorrect response that are correct, restate the question, rephrase questions, give hints or clues, or ask students to restate the answer.

- Make greater use of cooperative learning activities and structures to help students feel accepted by their peers and reinforce the power of group interaction and cooperation.

- Make a greater effort to compliment students on their positive behaviors, characteristics, and contributions.

(continued)

II. Helping Students Develop a Sense of Comfort and Order

A. Commendations

- You did an effective job of helping students develop a sense of personal comfort through the frequent and systematic use of activities involving some form of physical movement.

- You dignified students as learners and as co-participants in your classroom by appropriately acknowledging their personal standards for comfort and order.

- You effectively assisted students in bracketing, or blocking out, negative thoughts and feelings, decreasing their impact on classroom performance.

- You clearly and consistently communicated and reinforced classroom rules and procedures.

- You appeared to be consistently aware of and sensitive to the physical safety and well-being of your students, including the application of clear rules concerning teasing or threats.

B. Recommendations

- Be sensitive to the energy level of the students in your room. When that level appears to diminish, consider using one or more of the following techniques: ask students to bracket negative thoughts and feelings, allow for a short stretch break, or shift between independent and group activities.

- Periodically ask students to assess the extent to which they are keeping their personal space up to the standards they have established both individually and as a member of the classroom group.

- Work with students to help them bracket troublesome thoughts and feelings. For example, as Jaime Escalante suggests in the film *Stand and Deliver*, help students to "think cool" and to bracket out thoughts and emotions that keep them off task.

- Well-articulated classroom rules and procedures are a powerful way of conveying a sense of order to students. Explore options for helping students develop and maintain a more effective sense of order in your classroom by the use of strategies such as discussing with students the meaning and rationale for rules and procedures, providing students with a written list, posting rules and procedures in the classroom, role-playing, and modeling their use.

- The clearer you can be about policies regarding physical safety, the stronger the message will be to students. Policies and rules should include a description of the consequences of threatening or harming other students.

- Please pay greater attention to malicious teasing or threats made by students in your classroom; take steps to stop such harassment. Make sure your students know that you are looking out for their safety and well-being. Be sure that they understand you will take action on their behalf.

III. Helping Students Perceive Tasks as Valuable and Believe They Can Perform Tasks Successfully

A. Commendations

- Your enthusiasm and commitment to both your students and your subject matter consistently reinforced students' sense of academic trust in your classroom. All students appeared to be actively involved and excited about participating in the tasks you assigned.

- You did an excellent job of linking classroom tasks to students' personal interests and goals. By asking students to generate some of the tasks in which they were engaged, you dignified them as learners and you reinforced their ownership of the material.

- Your consistently positive feedback to students resulted in an extremely warm and supportive classroom climate throughout the lesson. You were particularly effective at specifying what students did to produce positive results.

(continued)

- When students were engaged in difficult or challenging activities, you consistently reinforced their ability to use positive self-talk, replacing negative self-talk with positive declarations and affirmations.

B. Recommendations

- Strive to exhibit a greater sense of enthusiasm and energy concerning the material you present. If you are excited about the content, students will pick up your enthusiasm.

- Whenever possible, work to make abstract ideas more concrete for students by using illustrative anecdotes and interesting asides related to the information being presented.

- Rather than maintaining continual control over assignment design, you might periodically modify some assignments to allow students to generate their own tasks to be performed in class or for homework.

- Whenever possible, strive to link classroom tasks to students' own interests and goals.

- Use more praising and acknowledging behaviors in your instructional delivery. For example, wherever appropriate, attribute students' successes to their personal efforts and specify and reinforce what students did that produced successful outcomes in your classroom.

- Many of your students exhibited self-defeating, negative self-talk behaviors in your classroom. Work with them to identify negative self-comments they make in specific situations and help them to change their behavior to positive self-talk and self-acknowledgment.

IV. Helping Students Understand and Be Clear About Tasks

A. Commendations

- You did an excellent job of identifying and articulating to students the specific behaviors you expected during and after completion of tasks.

- When students appeared to have trouble with a complex task, you did an extremely effective job of breaking it down into a series of smaller tasks for them.

- You displayed great sensitivity and commitment to your students as you helped to guide them through each step of the instructional tasks you assigned during the lesson.

- As students worked through the components of tasks you assigned, you were particularly adept at pointing out milestones necessary to complete the larger task.

- When reinforcing students' mastery of essential information and skills, you consistently specified situations in which you expected students to exhibit knowledge of this material.

B. Recommendations

- The clearer you can be about expected student performance on tasks, the more effective your instruction will be.

- Please be more explicit in explaining to students the situations in which you expect them to exhibit or apply knowledge of the material you are presenting.

- Provide students with models and examples of assignments you are requiring them to complete.

- If students appear to be having trouble with large, complex tasks, break them into a series of smaller tasks and guide them through successful completion of each one.

- Throughout a multi-step instructional activity, point out to students milestones or benchmarks necessary to complete the larger task.

(continued)

- To reinforce the relevance and purpose of an instructional activity, you might consider bringing in concrete items that relate to the abstractions being presented in class.
- Ask students to describe what they think you want them to do for classroom tasks. Use this input to correct student misconceptions or misunderstandings.

9

Professional Development and Observing Dimensions of Learning

Professional development is a critically important element of any successful learning organization. In order to remain viable, an organization must provide its staff with ongoing, meaningful opportunities for professional growth—opportunities that are sensitive to the unique needs of the adult learner. If instructors, administrators, and curriculum specialists are to internalize Dimensions of Learning and incorporate it effectively into their daily practice, staff development must reflect the following basic principles:

- Effective professional development is a cooperative process that grows from the expressed needs and talents of the individuals for whom it is designed.

- In the true learning organization, staff development empowers educators to examine critically their collective purpose and roles within an overall process of school transformation.

- Effective staff development cannot be imposed on the adult learner; he or she must elect to participate in it and view it as a meaningful vehicle for supporting professional and personal growth and awareness.

- No new strategy, technique, or educational process can be learned in a single session or practice opportunity. Meaningful and effective professional growth involves ongoing opportunities for rehearsing new behaviors, receiving effective coaching to perfect them, and using those behaviors in a risk-free environment.

- The techniques, principles, and processes for observing Dimensions of Learning (i.e., clinical supervision, cognitive coaching, peer coaching, and action research) cannot be mastered in traditional, one-shot, large-group staff development settings. Any effective professional growth program designed to facilitate staff mastery of these processes must include the use of coaching-based study groups and other vehicles that reinforce peer collaboration and shared inquiry.

Before looking at specific models and resources, it may be useful to review the thinking of current experts in the field of staff development. In the article "Nine Perspectives on the Future of Staff Development" (*Journal of Staff Development*, Winter 1991), nine national educational leaders express a vision for the design of 21st century professional growth experiences. The ideas presented in this article are consistent with the goals of a training program for observing Dimensions of Learning. For example, Mary Hatwood Futrell, former president of the National Educational Association, reminds us that

> the goal of staff development for America's educators must be nothing less than to transform human nature. Risk-taking must become the norm, not the exception. . . . Staff development must help the teaching profession move toward the day when every teacher is a visionary, an agitator, an agent of change, an enemy of stasis (p. 3).

Phil C. Schlechty, president of the Center for Leadership in School Reform and a well-recognized expert in the field of school restructuring and organizational transformation, emphasizes the critical role of productive mental habits as a key element in effective staff development:

> If teaching emerges as a leadership profession, the implications for staff development will be profound. Concern for technique (i.e., doing things right) will be replaced by concern for judgment (i.e., determining what is right to do). Instead of teacher training, we will be concerned with leadership development (p. 3).

An emphasis on developing educators' capacity for critical analysis, creativity, and self-regulated thinking is evident in the views of all nine educational leaders. Similarly, all of them emphasize the need to develop learning organizations, not just learning individuals. As Judson Hixson, Director of Professional Preparation and Development, North Central Regional Educational Lab, suggests,

> Staff development must become the process through which educators are enabled to thoughtfully and critically examine the purpose, role, structure, and organization of schooling in relation to the increasingly diverse students and communities they serve. Staff development must help schools move beyond simply improving what they have to developing understandings of what they need, new visions of what is possible, and new strategies for how best to 'get there from here' (p. 4).

Arthur L. Costa cautions us to view ourselves as "transformers" rather than "tinkerers," underscoring the contextual nature of effective staff development and reinforcing the essential processes needed for training staff to both implement and observe for Dimensions of Learning:

Staff developers must command a broader charge that includes skills of empowering the collaborative efforts of school staffs, community groups, administrators, legislators, and board members to:

- Envision the future as a basis for deriving educational goals, to continually clarify those goals, and to operationalize them into appropriate curriculum and instructional practices.

- Design action research employing a range of authentic assessment techniques to generate feedback for students to evaluate their own growth and for the teaching team to evaluate the effects of their instructional decisions.

- Recognize and abandon obsolete curriculum content and to purge incompatible school practices or policies so as to lodge these goals in every facet of the school culture.

- To assess their own growth toward and modeling of behaviors that are consistent with these goals of the new century (p. 6).

How can school systems and school staffs move toward creating a professional development program for observing Dimensions of Learning? How can staffs be true to the design principles proposed by such leaders in the field as Carl Glickman and Emily Calhoun of the University of Georgia, who remind us in the above-mentioned article that "internally controlled, participatory developed, site-based staff development programs linked to school goals are our best long-term answer to truly improving schools, but such programs will not always go smoothly (p. 7). Each system and school site must create a professional development program consistent with its unique goals, needs, and staff backgrounds. The materials presented in this book are models for use in initiating discussion and group exploration, but they are not intended as ends in themselves. For these materials to be meaningful, a learning organization may want to explore the following professional development questions:

- What is the nature of our current observation process?

- How successfully have we integrated Dimensions of Learning into the observation of teachers and their interactions with students?

- To what extent have we provided meaningful, ongoing training of our staff in the Dimensions of Learning model that includes opportunities to develop and implement unit plans consistent with the five dimensions?

- How have we restructured our curriculum, standards for teaching, and assessment programs to align them with Dimensions of Learning?

- How successfully have we created a collaborative approach to Dimensions of Learning implementation, including the use of study groups involving both teachers and administrators?

- What are our specific goals in training instructors, administrators, and curriculum specialists to observe for Dimensions of Learning?
- Do we have a long-term professional development plan to support our collective commitment to achieving these goals?

The suggestions described in the following section provide a starting point for exploring these issues. A school may choose to integrate the resources identified here into its Dimensions of Learning observation training plan. Or a school system may choose to use these resources to integrate Dimensions of Learning into a systemwide process of staff development. The resources may be especially useful in supporting efforts to align the implementation process with ongoing reform efforts in the areas of curriculum, instruction, assessment, and program evaluation.

Part I: Investigating the Learning Organization

A school or school system interested in integrating Dimensions of Learning into its overall approach to school reform might begin by exploring the idea of a learning organization, as Peter Senge defines it in his book *The Fifth Discipline (1990)*. ASCD has produced several videotape programs on professional development that can support a process of joint inquiry. The video program *Shared Decision Making* (ASCD 1993a), for example, includes a 30-minute tape titled "Changing Schools Through Shared Decision Making" that models a process for (1) developing school plans based on ideas from staff members who are likely to know what will work, (2) creating a democratic process for making decisions, and (3) improving the day-to-day culture of the school. The second 30-minute tape in this program, "Shared Decision Making: How It Works," presents a behind-the-scenes view of site-based management at a school in which shared decision making is characterized by new roles and responsibilities, staff development in the use of new skills, and consensus building.

For those interested in a brief but powerful overview of the Total Quality Movement and its relationship to the learning organization, ASCD also offers an excellent 30-minute videotape program called *Schools of Quality* (ASCD 1993c). The program takes the viewer into one elementary and one middle school in a large suburban school district to see the dramatic impact that the Quality philosophy has had on these schools. Consistent with the principles of the learning organization—and critical to the success of Dimensions of Learning implementation—this overview stresses how a school or school system can learn to focus on the needs of the children and the community, develop a broad-based commitment to continuous improvement, examine their school system objectively through data collection and "systems pictures" of their organizations and processes, and sustain change through a commitment from leadership.

Issues related to integrating curriculum and redesigning assessments to align them with Dimensions of Learning can be addressed using a variety of professional development programs available through ASCD, including *Integrating the Curriculum* (ASCD 1993b), *Outcome-Based Education* (ASCD 1992c), and *Redesigning Assessment* (ASCD 1992d), an overview of new trends in monitoring student progress. Similarly, the videotape program *Involving Parents in Education* (ASCD 1992b) is an excellent starting point for exploring how parents and community members can help schools address problems that inevitably surface during the process of organizational change. Each of these resources complements study group and school improvement team investigations of key issues related to the learning organization. They are also rich sources for identifying print materials that can be read and discussed by team members.

Part II: Exploring the Observation Process

For the school or school system seeking to transform its observation process, several additional videotape programs are available. Perhaps the most detailed and complete overview of the contemporary observation process is the five-tape series *Another Set of Eyes: Techniques for Classroom Observation* (ASCD 1989b) and *Another Set of Eyes: Conferencing Skills* (ASCD 1989a). Used with the materials in this book, Another Set of Eyes offers a comprehensive approach to observation that can be easily adopted by clinical supervisors and peer coaches for observing and recording student/teacher interactions in the classroom. The tapes include viewer-friendly explanations of observation techniques, as well as demonstrations by experienced teachers and teacher supervisors showing how those techniques help teachers reflect on their classroom practices.

Adapting the suggestions for observing Dimensions of Learning presented in this book, educators can benefit greatly from exploring the six observation techniques presented in *Another Set of Eyes*. These techniques can give teachers the objective data they need to improve both their interactions with students and their ability to employ effective strategies from the DoL model. The observation techniques include

- Selective verbatim—providing teachers with information about their verbal behaviors, such as how well they use questions to stimulate student learning.

- Verbal flow—describing objectively the teacher/student verbal interaction in the classroom and showing the teacher which students participate in class discussions.

- At task—giving teachers information about student at-task behavior that they would not receive otherwise.

- Class traffic—showing teacher movement around the class in an objective way that illustrates how effectively teachers manage all the students in the class, especially in active classes such as industrial arts, science labs, or art classes.

- Interaction analysis—giving teachers comprehensive data that reveal the patterns of interactions with students.

- Global scan—Providing ways to give general feedback on teaching behavior in a caring, informative way.

This videotape series also profiles conferencing skills that can help motivate teachers to make long-term, positive changes in their instructional behavior. In observing for Dimensions of Learning, the clinical supervisor or peer coach can easily incorporate the following pre-conference, observation, and post-observation interactions to reinforce desired outcomes for instructional change: *trust-building skills* (techniques for using both verbal and nonverbal interactions to reinforce effective communication and build rapport); *questioning skills* (using a variety of question frames and techniques to help teachers make effective decisions related to the improvement of students' thinking processes); *responding skills* (requesting specifics, helping teachers envision lesson outcomes, and using paraphrasing to clarify objectives); and *empowering skills* (exploring teachers' motivation by asking them to use previous experience in decision making, consider alternatives, and be specific). The observer can use these techniques to help teachers improve instruction and student performance.

Another video series, *Opening Doors: An Introduction to Peer Coaching* (ASCD 1989c), is a clear, straightforward overview of the peer coaching process in its various forms. Dimensions of Learning study groups can use this two-tape program to reinforce for themselves and the rest of the staff the benefits of peer coaching, including the improvement of morale and motivation, promoting better teaching in an environment in which ideas are exchanged, and ensuring that training transfers from workshops to classroom practice. Reinforcing the clinical supervision elements of pre-conferencing, observing, and post-conferencing, the tapes provide examples of teacher/coach interactions that improve instruction and enhance team building: *mirroring*, in which the coach records but does not interpret the data the teacher has requested; *collaborative coaching*, in which teacher and coach work together to find ways to improve teaching; and *expert coaching*, in which the coach acts as a mentor, giving specific suggestions to the teacher.

Finally, school staffs interested in incorporating action research into their Dimensions of Learning implementation process should explore the four-part series *Action Research: Inquiry, Reflection, and Decision Making* (ASCD 1995). This detailed overview explores how collaborative investigation at the site level can support the school's ability to become a learning organization. Participants see action research in operation at a variety of sites across the United States, with research teams using the process to identify and solve problems in the classroom and throughout the school. Demonstrating the five-phase process of action research—selecting a focus, collecting data, organizing data, analyzing and interpreting data, and taking action—the videotaped case studies include an elementary school, a junior high school, and a systemwide application. These scenarios parallel the four levels of Dimensions of Learning implementation, including issues related to improving curriculum and instruction, creating more positive learning environments, and guiding districtwide improvement efforts.

Part III: Observing Dimensions of Learning

In addition to viewing the six-tape *Dimensions of Learning Videotape Package* (ASCD 1992a), staffs interested in using the materials in this book as a basis for formal training should explore two other resource collections: *The Teaching Strategies Library* (ASCD 1987/1989) and *The Video Library of Teaching Episodes* (ASCD 1988). The first collection consists of eight strategy tapes that emphasize techniques and interventions consistent with the design principles and components of Dimensions of Learning. Individual tapes in the series are titled "Mastery Lecture," "Concept Attainment," "Concept Formation," "Peer Practice," "Compare and Contrast," "Reading for Meaning," "Synectics," and "Circle of Knowledge."

The second series contains over 30 videotaped teaching episodes that serve as an excellent resource for clinical supervisors, cognitive and peer coaches, and action research teams interested in observing at a school site or system level. Although both resources offer numerous opportunities for applying the materials and suggestions in this book, I have summarized below five specific examples of how to use these videotapes to train educators to look for and evaluate the effectiveness of key Dimensions of Learning components and strategies during the observation process.

For each of the videotaped episodes described below, trainers may wish to use the introductory resource "Observing for Dimensions of Learning: A Sweep' Through the Territory" (Figure 9.1 on pp. 111–112). This observation checklist is a brief, user-friendly outline of key teacher behaviors associated with each of the five dimensions. Workshop participants might be asked to observe for one or more of the dimension descriptors, taking running notes on what they observe to support their observations and conclusions.

Also included for each of the videotaped teaching episodes are additional DoL guide questions specifically tied to that episode. Training groups, peer coaching teams, and DoL study groups are strongly encouraged to use these introductory resources as a starting point. When groups reach a certain level of knowledge, comfort, and expertise, they may want to use the more extensive materials included at the end of each of the previous chapters, as these materials will help school staff practice post-observation conferencing techniques and develop post-observation written feedback.

Suggested Teaching Episode One. "An Overview of Dimensions of Learning in Action: Third-Grade Reading and Writing Preparation Strategies" (episode 25 of the ASCD *Video Library of Teaching Episodes*). In this videotape, we see Sherry Schreiber of Troost Communications and Writing Academy, Kansas City, Missouri, working with a group of 3rd graders to develop a class "big book" describing some of their experiences with relatives. This tape is an excellent resource for introducing staffs to the five dimensions of learning in a classroom setting.

In this episode, Ms. Schreiber demonstrates all five of the dimensions of learning. She creates a vibrant, nurturing classroom climate and culture (Dimension 1); articulates key outcomes to students so that they all understand what they are expected to know and be able to do as a result of the lesson (Dimension 2); facilitates students' ability to compare, classify, infer, predict, elaborate, and analyze perspectives (Dimension 3); supports students in working independently to contribute to a whole-class meaningful-use task (Dimension 4); and continually reinforces students' productive mental habits, including their ability to remain self-regulated, creative, and critical in their thinking operations (Dimension 5).

In addition to using the "Sweep Through the Territory" overview, training groups might also benefit from discussing the following questions concerning Ms. Schreiber's lesson:

- How does the instructor establish and continue to reinforce a warm, nurturing climate in her classroom? Cite specific examples of how her students are encouraged to feel good about themselves as learners, as members of a team, and as capable workers who clearly understand the task(s) assigned to them?

- How does Ms. Schreiber introduce and reinforce essential declarative and procedural knowledge in the lesson? Cite examples of Dimension 2 strategies that contribute to students' ability to understand and internalize key lesson objectives (e.g., cooperative learning structures, role playing, sensory experiences, Before-During-After strategies, or coaching for skills development).

- During the reading process, how are students supported in extending and refining their knowledge? How does the design of Ms. Schreiber's questions and related instructional activities reinforce students' ability to compare, classify, predict, infer, deduce, elaborate, identify errors, and compare perspectives?

- This lesson is the first in a series in which Ms. Schreiber prepares her students to contribute to a meaningful-use task being worked on by the class. What is this meaningful-use task and how does it reflect Dimensions of Learning design principles?

- Throughout this episode, how does Ms. Schreiber encourage her students to reflect on their own thinking through the use of metacognitive techniques? How does she reinforce key habits of mind related to self-regulated, critical, and creative thinking?

Suggested Teaching Episode Two. "Second-Grade Language Arts Story Writing" (episode 23 of the ASCD *Video Library of Teaching Episodes*). In this episode, Ann Williams of the Dr. Bernard Harris Sr. Elementary School, Baltimore, Maryland, uses a wide variety of introductory experiences to review with her students the folk heroes from tall tales and other stories they have studied. Beginning with a series of props and costumes taken from a set of "mystery bags," Ms. Williams asks her students to dress up like certain folk heroes and heroines and recap what the class remembers about them. She then works with the students to develop original tall tales that they will share with one another.

In observing Ms. Williams and her class, study groups and training teams may wish to consider the following questions:

- What are the specific Dimension 1 strategies and techniques Ms. Williams uses to reinforce a positive and orderly classroom climate? How do such strategies as "silent clapping" contribute to students' positive attitudes and perceptions about learning?

- How does Ms. Williams introduce her students to key learning outcomes? At the conclusion of the lesson, how successfully have students achieved the objectives established for that lesson? What evidence can you present to confirm your conclusions?

- How successfully do students in Ms. Williams class extend and refine their use of essential declarative and procedural knowledge? In a post-observation conference, what commendations and recommendations might you make concerning Dimension 3 strategies and techniques?

- What suggestions might you make about how to align this lesson with a long-range, meaningful-use task? How might such a task be used to provide an effective conclusion for the students' unit on the tall tale?

Suggested Teaching Episode Three. "Writing a Complex Problem" (episode 29 of the ASCD *Video Library of Teaching Episodes*). While the first two episodes emphasize reading and writing activities at the elementary level, this episode features Ed Cannon of T. C. Williams High School, Alexandria, Virginia, leading a group of 10th-grade English students through the development of a problem-based writing assignment. Like his elementary counterparts, Mr. Cannon uses a variety of Dimensions of Learning strategies to maintain a climate of success for all students. Building on students' recent reading of Steinbeck's novel *The Pearl,* he makes a concerted effort to encourage peer interaction, elicit student experiences that parallel aspects of the writing assignment, and reinforce the value of relating what students are learning to their own lives. In observing Mr. Cannon and his students, training groups might use the following questions to inform their own observation process:

- Cite ways in which Mr. Cannon creates a classroom climate that invites active student participation and input.

- How does the instructor attempt to integrate students' personal experiences and perceptions with the ideas and themes presented in Steinbeck's novel?

- How does Mr. Cannon support his students in acquiring and integrating essential declarative and procedural knowledge throughout the lesson?

- Are there specific Dimension 3 extending and refining strategies that are used effectively in this episode? Which others might you recommend to enhance students' ability to extend and refine their knowledge?

- Would you describe the student's writing task as a Dimension 4 meaningful-use task? If so, why? If not, what recommendations could you make to Mr. Cannon for teaching Dimension 4 skills?

- What commendations and recommendations might you make concerning the instructor's reinforcement of students' understanding and use of important mental habits?

Suggested Teaching Episode Four. "Metaphorical Problem Solving" (episode 14 of the ASCD *Video Library of Teaching Episodes*). Both this episode and the one that follows are particularly useful to educators who are observing for Dimension 3. In this lesson on metaphorical problem solving, Joan Bailey of Hawthorne Elementary School, Teaneck, New Jersey, leads her students through the Synectics process, helping students explore analogies that create unusual and creative comparisons to the solar system. Ms. Bailey is particularly effective at encouraging all her students to be actively engaged in exploring a series of metaphors.

Using the four-part Synectics framework, Ms. Bailey begins with a teacher-generated analogy, asking students to brainstorm ways in which the solar system is like an orchestra. She then asks them to imagine how the solar system and the planets might feel if they were an orchestra, after which they are asked to cite ways in which the two entities are dissimilar. Finally, Ms. Bailey asks students to create an original metaphor comparing the solar system to some other thing of their choice, citing reasons for their decision.

This episode can help elementary and middle school study groups explore how Dimension 3 techniques manifest in a classroom setting. The following questions may support this aspect of the DoL observation process:

- How does Ms. Bailey elicit enthusiasm and involvement from her students at the beginning of the teaching episode? How does she use peer interaction, including cooperative learning teams, to reinforce students' knowledge and involvement?

- How does the instructor's introduction of the lesson objectives reinforce active student involvement and participation?

- What commendations and recommendations can you cite regarding Ms. Bailey's use of the Synectics process to assist students in extending and refining their knowledge of the solar system? Consider the four components: presenting a teacher-generated analogy, asking students to "become" the analogy by imagining how it would feel, negating the analogy, and facilitating student-generated metaphors.

- What would you say to Ms. Bailey in a post-observation conference? What written commendations and recommendations might you include in post-observation follow-ups?

- What suggestions might you offer Ms. Bailey concerning how students' participation in this Synectics lesson could be integrated into a culminating meaningful-use task at the conclusion of their unit on the solar system?

Suggested Teaching Episode Five. "Synthesis/Synectics" (ASCD *Teaching Strategies Library, Part 2*). For study groups and training teams interested in a high school model for observing Dimension 3, this 15-minute lesson (mid-point in the videotape) is ideal. It features Nancy Hawkins and her 10th-grade biology students at Visalia High School, Visalia, California, as they review their work on the circulatory system. The lesson begins with an excellent example of how sensory experiences can reinforce students' understanding of essential declarative knowledge. We see Ms. Hawkins' students "become" the circulatory system, with students playing the part of the blood, cells, and veins.

Using the four-part Synectics process, Ms. Hawkins begins by asking her students to think of ways in which the circulatory system might be compared to a toy railroad. They imagine how the circulatory system might feel if it were a toy railroad, then explore ways in which the analogy might not be apt. Finally, the students choose an alternative analogy and create an impressive display of graphic representations that compare the circulatory system to the analogy they have chosen.

Secondary training and study groups might consider the following questions as they view this teaching episode:

- How does the hands-on sensory experience featured at the beginning of the videotaped lesson prepare students for the Synectics activities that follow?

- What essential declarative and procedural knowledge must the students use and apply as they work through this lesson? Based on your observation, how successfully have Ms. Hawkins' students acquired and integrated this knowledge?

- Although Synectics activities emphasize the Dimension 3 thinking skill of comparison, what other cognitive skills do Ms. Hawkins' students use? For example, how effectively do they extend and refine their knowledge through induction and deduction activities? How does Ms. Hawkins encourage them to analyze perspectives, identify errors, generate abstract patterns, and create supporting evidence?

- In a post-observation conference, what commendations and recommendations would you give Ms. Hawkins concerning her use of Dimension 3 strategies and techniques?

Using these videotaped episodes and the related questions represents only one avenue for administrators and teachers to reinforce their skills in observing for Dimensions of Learning. The materials and suggestions in this book are most helpful when applied directly to live teaching episodes. In order to master the observation techniques, it is important to observe the teaching practices of educators at the school site itself. For the adventurous and committed, these strategies and materials are best applied to the study of videotaped lessons taught by the school's peer coaching or training group.

FIGURE 9.1
Observing for Dimensions of Learning:
A "Sweep" Through the Territory

To reinforce your knowledge of how to observe for Dimensions of Learning, use the following outline to observe each selected videotaped teaching episode. On your own, check those elements you observe during the lesson. At the end of the lesson, compare your choices with those of your partner or small group. Discuss observation data that confirm your decisions.

I. DIMENSION 1: Helping Students Develop Positive Attitudes and Perceptions About Learning

_____ A. The instructor helps all students feel accepted.

_____ B. The instructor helps all students develop a sense of comfort in the classroom.

_____ C. The instructor has designed instruction so that it reinforces students' sense of order in the classroom.

_____ D. The instructor helps students clearly understand assigned tasks.

_____ E. The instructor helps students believe that they have the ability and resources to successfully complete assigned tasks .

NOTES:

II. DIMENSION 2: Helping Students Acquire and Integrate Knowledge

_____ A. The instructor has designed instruction to help students construct meaning for declarative knowledge (i.e., facts, concepts, generalizations, principles) through the use of a variety of interactive strategies.

_____ B. Students receive support to organize and store declarative knowledge effectively.

_____ C. The instructor introduces and reinforces essential procedural knowledge (i.e., skills, processes, procedures) through ongoing modeling, shaping, and internalizing that include providing extensive practice opportunities.

NOTES:

III. DIMENSION 3: Helping Students Extend and Refine Knowledge

_____ A. Wherever appropriate, students receive instructional support to "own" essential knowledge through activities requiring thoughtful application.

_____ B. The instructors' questions focus on higher-level thinking skills and processes, rather than exclusive emphasis on knowledge/recall.

(continued)

_____ C. Students receive support to understand and apply important thinking processes such as the following:

_____ Comparison	_____ Analyzing errors
_____ Classification	_____ Constructing support
_____ Induction	_____ Abstracting/pattern recognition
_____ Deduction	_____ Analysis of perspectives

NOTES:

IV. DIMENSION 4: Meaningful Use of Knowledge

_____ A. Where appropriate, the instructor involves students in long-term, self-directed, experience-based learning activities that reflect real-world roles and situations.

_____ B. Where appropriate, the instructor engages students in meaningful-use tasks designed to reinforce their ability to use the following thinking operations:

_____ Decision making	_____ Experimental inquiry
_____ Problem solving	_____ Invention
_____ Investigation	

NOTES:

V. DIMENSION 5: Developing and Using Productive Habits of Mind

_____ A. The instructor models effective thinking skills and behaviors.

_____ B. The instructor encourages students to reflect on their own thinking and monitor their own comprehension.

_____ C. The instructor has designed classroom activities to reinforce students' ability to be self-regulated in their thinking, including planning, use of resources, sensitivity to feedback, and evaluating the effectiveness of their own actions.

_____ D. The instructor encourages students to be effective critical thinkers, including seeking accuracy and clarity, being open-minded, and restraining impulsivity.

_____ E. The instructor encourages students to be creative, to express their own opinions, to push the limits of their knowledge, and to generate new ways of viewing a situation.

NOTES:

10

One School System's Story

The ideas and suggestions presented in this book are more than abstractions: They extend from my experiences as a member of the Dimensions of Learning implementation team in the Prince George's County Public Schools in Maryland. All of the materials have been field-tested by the administrators and teachers of that school system. This chapter is a summary of our system's DoL implementation process, including the role that the strategies and materials presented here played in that process.

What I hope will be of particular interest to systems just beginning to work with Dimensions of Learning is the way we modified two of our major curriculum components: (1) Directed Teaching Activity, our systemwide model for lesson planning based on Madeline Hunter's work described in *Mastery Teaching* (1982); and (2) "Standards for Excellence in Teaching," our systemwide description of instructional standards and indicators that guides and informs much of our formal teacher observation and evaluation process (Figures 10.1 and 10.2, which appear later in the chapter).

Maryland was the first state in the United States to adopt Dimensions of Learning for statewide dissemination and implementation. Through the work of Jay McTighe, one of the authors of *Assessing Student Outcomes: Performance Assessment Using the Dimensions of Learning Model* (Marzano, Pickering, and McTighe 1993), and other Maryland State Department of Education personnel, a group of potential trainers participated in four-day Dimensions of Learning workshops offered throughout the state.

Following the workshops, which were conducted by Debra Pickering during the 1991–92 academic year, each of the 24 Maryland public school systems was encouraged to incorporate the Dimensions of Learning program into its strategic plan for addressing the learning outcomes and standards identified by the Maryland State Department of Education and the State Board of Education.

Prince George's County Public Schools is now actively involved in full-system adoption and implementation of the Dimensions of Learning program. DoL is an invaluable part of our school system's response to the Maryland School Performance Program, a statewide accountability initiative that emphasizes the development of students' higher-order thinking skills and includes the use of the School-Based Instructional Decision-Making Process (SBIDM). SBIDM is a commitment to allowing school staffs to make decisions concerning their budget, instructional delivery system, and school site governance and management.

Our school system was fortunate to become one of four state SBIDM professional development centers, an opportunity that allowed us to design our plan for implementing Dimensions of Learning systemwide. Through a state-funded SBIDM grant, our diverse urban system—with a population of 111,132; 76.5% minority enrollment; and 81 native languages among a growing language minority—has implemented an ambitious Dimensions of Learning training and curriculum development program that has included

- Five two-day training sessions for three instructors from every elementary and middle school and four instructors from every high school.
- Multiple half- and full-day training sessions for all school administrators.
- One-day training sessions for all supervisors and administrators in the Departments of Curriculum and Instruction, Staff Development, Special Education, Personnel, Pupil Services, and Library Media and Technology Resources.
- A variety of site-based, full-staff training programs conducted by system trainers.
- State-approved workshops, which provided one to three credits toward recertification.
- A systemwide commitment to the integration of Dimensions of Learning strategies and principles into all facets of curriculum development.

Prince George's County Public Schools' first major initiative was a two-day seminar conducted by district trainers for members of the Thinking Connection, an oversight committee composed of administrators and instructional specialists with a particular interest in the field of thinking skills improvement. Using feedback from this preliminary session, the trainers, under the supervision of the Department of Staff Development, created a two-day training model to be offered to teams from every elementary, middle, and high school in the county. A two-day workshop was conducted for each of the five administrative areas in the school system. Participating teams were encouraged to work with their administrators and School Improvement Teams to develop follow-up plans for their schools. Combined with a variety of long-term, site-based training programs (offered after school and during team planning periods), approximately two-thirds of the system's educators have received some type of formal training in Dimensions of Learning.

In addition, the system has instituted an unusual and significant training component that reflects its commitment to the use of Dimensions of Learning to guide and inform our efforts to improve students' thinking skills. For the first time in its history, the school system has offered special half- and full-day workshops for virtually every major department. Personnel supervisors, for example, have examined the implications of the program for new teacher recruitment, candidate profiles, and related hiring practices. Members of the Department of Special Education (including principals and wing coordinators of Special Centers) have explored the implications of the program for special education students. The Department of Pupil Services has examined the relationship of Dimensions of Learning to guidance and related student services. Similar workshops have involved instructional supervisors and specialists, library media specialists, and school administrators. To lend support and credibility to administrator trainings, principals are conducting the workshops and highlighting the ways in which they are integrating the program into their school improvement plans.

In moving beyond Level 1 and Level 2 implementation (described in Chapter 2), the system has redesigned many of its key curriculum support documents. In addition, the observation materials included in this book have been used to train administrators and instructional supervisors and specialists in how to integrate Dimensions of Learning into their teacher observation and evaluation processes. All of the system's new curriculum guides, for example, have integrated the major unit design principles from Dimensions of Learning, with particular emphasis on ensuring that students move toward independent application of productive mental habits in the context of meaningful-use tasks. Each of these elements was developed as part of the commitment to systemwide implementation at Levels 3 and Level 4.

At Level 3, experienced teachers and instructional supervisors and specialists are provided with guided practice in using the Dimensions of Learning unit planning guides to design new units of instruction. Within the school system, the focus on performance-based instructional design has provided powerful opportunities to prepare students for the integrated, performance-based assessments they encounter as part of the Maryland School Performance Assessment Program.

At Level 4, Dimensions of Learning becomes a framework for restructuring—a systemwide catalyst for change in curriculum, instruction, and assessment. It is toward this final level that DoL initiatives are now directed as part of a long-term process of curriculum alignment, emphasis on authentic instruction, and expansion of testing and evaluation techniques to stress performance assessment.

The preliminary results of this initiative have been impressive. Evidence suggests that we are making progress toward achieving our commitment to Level 4 implementation. Perhaps most importantly, Dimensions of Learning has had an impact on student achievement. While the impact of DoL can be felt throughout the school system, the following represents at least a partial summary of its influence to this point:

1. Strong evidence is now available of improved student performance in those schools that have achieved Level 4 implementation status:

- Many schools in the system have involved teachers actively in Dimensions of Learning lesson and unit plan design to complement their instructional program. Particular successes are evident in Level 4 sites where teachers have used DoL design principles to create performance-based assessment tasks consistent with state accountability testing.

- In elementary and middle schools that have achieved Level 4 implementation status, significant improvement is evident in student's Maryland School Performance Assessment Program scores, especially in those tasks that assess Dimension 3, extending and refining knowledge.

- In high schools that have achieved Level 4 implementation status, evidence exists that social studies teachers using DoL strategies have helped improve students' performance on the Maryland Test of Citizenship skills. This test, which is required for graduation, contains a vast number of declarative, knowledge-based questions about U.S. federal, state, and local government. Dimension 2 strategies have proven highly effective in helping students construct meaning and organize and store essential knowledge assessed on the test.

2. There is now a systemwide commitment to designing curriculum that is coherent and strategic in its emphasis on improving students' ability to think:

- School system staff have developed a new series of scope-and-sequence documents to identify the system's core curriculum, key indicators of student performance, and ways to integrate Dimensions of Learning into every discipline and program.

- Strategies and learning experiences consistent with the Dimensions of Learning program are now present in all written curriculum materials, including evidence of increased performance-based activities consistent with Dimension 4.

- In addition to curriculum guides, administrators have developed new curriculum support documents to articulate the relationship between Dimensions of Learning and statewide accountability tests. Increasingly there is less emphasis on teaching for the test and more emphasis on designing and implementing active, student-centered learning experiences that support students' ability to demonstrate productive mental habits during testing situations.

3. In all Level 4 DoL implementation sites, instructional repertoires have changed as a result of renewed staff commitment to collaborative inquiry and school-based instructional decision making:

- Teachers in these sites have begun to form peer coaching and support teams to develop and implement DoL lesson and unit plans.

- Teachers have expanded their instructional techniques to include many more performance-based instructional tasks that involve students in active, inquiry-based learning with real-world applications.

- Level 4 implementation sites include a growing number of cooperative learning activities.

- A majority of Level 4 sites have begun to make tremendous progress toward using integrated and interdisciplinary instructional designs.

- Staff members have formed action research teams to study the Dimensions of Learning implementation process and to address emerging, related issues and problems at specific school sites.

4. Dimensions of Learning has provided a common language and methodology for school improvement and strategic planning at a majority of school sites:

- Each of these sites has now incorporated DoL into its school improvement plan, making it a major catalyst for long-range strategic change.

- Administrators and teachers have revised the teacher observation process to incorporate Dimensions of Learning commendations and recommendations.

- Increasingly, on-site experts (teachers who have used DoL to transform their own classrooms) are conducting the DoL trainings. Instead of central office staff dominating training delivery, educators are designing more and more of the training sessions to accommodate the unique needs of their students, staff, and organization.

- All teachers new to the system now receive training in Dimensions of Learning; the program has become a vehicle for articulating those instructional practices proven more successful in improving student academic performance.

5. Dimensions of Learning has been instrumental in transforming the assessment paradigm that operates in the school system:

- Performance assessment is becoming an important part of all teachers' repertoire for monitoring student progress.

- Increasingly, we see less evidence of strict reliance on traditional forms of testing and growing reliance on alternative approaches, including performance-based assessment tasks, portfolio assessment, and project-based summative assessment.

- School system criterion-referenced tests now include performance-based components in addition to traditional items such as multiple-choice formats.

- There is a growing dialogue in the system about how testing and the overall assessment program (including revised report card formats at both elementary and secondary levels) can enhance a systemwide commitment to improving students' thinking.

As the following materials show, the commitment to Level 4 implementation is felt most powerfully in documents that communicate to both new and senior teachers the standards and instructional indicators used to evaluate daily classroom activities. Consider, for example, how the system's Directed Teaching Activity (DTA) has been modified (Figure 10.1). Originally a synthesis of the lesson elements identified by Madeline Hunter (1982), the new DTA now has an interrogative tone rather than an imperative one: teachers are asked to consider a series of key design questions as they create daily lesson plans.

Perhaps more importantly, the observation checklist, "Standards for Excellence in Teaching" (Figure 10.2, p. 122), which overviews instructional standards and performance indicators, now emphasizes Dimensions of Learning unit planning suggestions and guidelines. In the Prince George's County Public Schools, six core standards areas have been identified to encompass what we call the "characteristics of effective teaching": (1) planning and preparation, (2) knowledge, (3) classroom management and organization, (4) classroom climate, (5) the process of instruction, and (6) outcomes of instruction. The revised checklist reinforces the principle of applying those standards to unit and lesson plan development and situating daily lessons within a carefully organized unit design that culminates in students' ability to work independently on meaningful-use tasks. Appendix A on page 125 contains a detailed set of suggestions and examples called "Integrating Dimensions of Learning into the Formal Teacher Observation Process." This document outlines problems and recommendations for each of the six standards areas.

Figure 10.1
Elements of An Effective Lesson
(Directed Teaching Activity)

Planning Guide

FOCUSING STUDENT ATTENTION (warm up): *How will I establish an anticipatory set to focus students' learning and to ensure on-task behavior by all students?*

- What will I do to help students develop positive attitudes and perceptions about the learning climate and the learning task?
- What brief task (up to 5 minutes) can I use to focus students' attention and prepare them to think critically?
- What brief task can I use to give students meaningful opportunities for practice of a key skill (i.e., procedural knowledge) or application of essential declarative knowledge?

_____

_____

_____

STATEMENT OF OBJECTIVE: *How will essential learner outcomes for the lesson be stated and communicated to students?*

- What do I want students to know and be able to do as a result of the lesson?
- How will I share the lesson objective(s) with my students?
- What is the primary instructional focus of my lesson:
    - Mastery of essential declarative and procedural knowledge?
    - Extension and refinement of essential knowledge?
    - Meaningful use of knowledge?
    - Demonstration of productive habits of mind?

_____

_____

_____

(continued)

INTRODUCTORY AND DEVELOPMENT ACTIVITIES (Teacher-directed): *How will I organize the lesson to ensure student mastery of essential learner outcomes? How will I integrate assessment of student progress into my instruction?*

Declarative Knowledge: What are the general topics and specifics of the lesson? What are the essential facts, concepts, generalizations, and principles that I wish to emphasize in the lesson?

- How will I help students construct meaning, organize information, and store it in long-term memory?
- How will students experience the information presented in the lesson?
- How will I help students to understand the value and relevance of the content and activities?
- Which mental habits will I introduce, emphasize, and/or reinforce?

_____

_____

_____

Procedural Knowledge: What skills, processes, competencies, and procedures do students really need to master in this lesson?

- How will I model the skills and processes in the lesson? How will I help students comprehend and use the skill or competency?
- How will I help students shape the skills and processes in the lesson?
- How will I help students internalize the skills and processes in the lesson?
- What mental habits will I introduce, emphasize, and/or reinforce?

_____

_____

_____

GUIDED PRACTICE ACTIVITIES (Teacher-monitored): *How will I help students extend and refine the declarative and procedural knowledge they are acquiring?*

- What information will I expect students to extend and refine?
- What activities will I provide to help students extend and refine their knowledge? To what extent will I use student-centered activities? To what extent will I use cooperative learning structures?
- Which extending and refining thinking processes are most appropriate for this particular lesson—comparison, classification, induction, deduction, error analysis, analysis of perspectives, abstraction, and/or constructing support?

_____

_____

_____

(continued)

INDEPENDENT ACTIVITIES/MEANINGFUL-USE TASKS (Student alone or in cooperative learning groups): *To what extent does this lesson contribute to students' ability to respond successfully to long-term, performance-based, meaningful-use tasks?*

- What independent activities and tasks are to be a part of this lesson?
- How do these activities and tasks reinforce students' mastery of essential learning outcomes?
- To what extent, if any, do these activities and tasks contribute to students' individual or collective response to an ongoing meaningful-use task that involves decision making, problem solving, investigation, experimental inquiry, and/or invention?

_____

_____

_____

ASSESSMENT ACTIVITIES: *Throughout the lesson, how will I monitor student progress?*

- What strategies will I use to monitor the extent of students' mastery of identified learner outcomes?
- What formative assessment strategies will I use to ensure that student progress is monitored from the beginning to the end of the lesson?
- What summative assessment strategy or strategies will I use to ensure that all students have mastered the essential learner outcomes?
- How will I integrate metacognitive strategies into my assessment process so that students can express and monitor their own comprehension and assess themselves as learners?
- How will I balance my assessment strategies to include both oral and written communication skills?

_____

_____

_____

CLOSURE ACTIVITY (Teacher-guided): *What activity will foster a sense of completion among student participants? Will it be a part of the assessment process, or will it function as a stand-alone activity?*

- How did we do?
- How far will we go tomorrow? For our next lesson, think about . . .
- In your opinion, what are the most significant or interesting parts of the lesson?
- How does the lesson relate to you and the world you inhabit?

_____

_____

_____

FIGURE 10.2
Standards for Excellence in Teaching
Observation Checklist

This checklist, which incorporates Dimensions of Learning strategies and techniques, is provided to assist the observer in reviewing his or her classroom observation notes and preparing for the post-observation conference with the teacher.

I. PLANNING AND PREPARATION
_____ A. The teacher prepared a written plan for instruction.
_____ B. The teacher used a specific task or activity to focus students' attention.
_____ C. The objective of the lesson was clear, specific, and communicated to students.
_____ D. The lesson plan contained a clear instructional focus, such as mastery of essential declarative and procedural knowledge, extension and refinement of knowledge, meaningful use of knowledge, or reinforcement of productive mental habits.

Comments/Notes:

II. KNOWLEDGE
_____ A. The teacher provided for the rates and learning styles of all students.
_____ B. The teacher used students' names, interacted with students, and provided positive verbal and nonverbal feedback.
_____ C. The teacher selected and modeled techniques and strategies to develop students' critical thinking skills.
_____ D. The teacher used effective questioning techniques and emphasized higher-order thinking skills rather than passive knowledge/recall of information.

Comments/Notes:

(*continued*)

III. CLASSROOM MANAGEMENT AND ORGANIZATION

_____ A. The teacher organized the classroom well and carefully managed student behavior.

_____ B. There were a variety and an appropriate quantity of materials of instruction.

_____ C. The teacher managed time well, allowing for maximum time devoted to successful learning experiences.

_____ D. The teacher demonstrated the ability to work with individuals, small groups, and large groups; where appropriate, he or she used cooperative learning structures to reinforce students' acquisition of essential declarative and procedural knowledge.

Comments/Notes:

IV. CLASSROOM CLIMATE

_____ A. The teacher consistently incorporated Dimension 1 techniques to create a positive and productive classroom climate that helped students feel accepted, perceive academic tasks as valuable and relevant to their lives, and believe that they have the ability and resources to perform challenging academic tasks.

_____ B. The classroom environment invited learning and helped students to develop a sense of comfort and order.

_____ C. The teacher reflected the attitude that all students can learn.

_____ D. The teacher provided displays related to the subject area that reinforced key learning.

_____ E. The classroom was clean and orderly.

Comments/Notes:

V. THE PROCESS OF INSTRUCTION

_____ A. The teacher organized introductory and developmental activities to ensure student mastery of key learner outcomes.

_____ B. Activities designed to reinforce essential declarative knowledge (i.e., essential facts, concepts, generalizations, and principles) helped students construct meaning, organize information, and store it in long-term memory .

_____ C. Activities designed to reinforce essential procedural knowledge (i.e. skills, processes, competencies, and procedures) included teacher modeling of the skill or process and numerous opportunities for students to practice, shape, and internalize the skill or process.

(continued)

_____ D. The teacher helped students to extend and refine declarative and procedural knowledge through direct and indirect instruction of the key thinking processes: comparison, classification, induction, deduction, error analysis, analysis of perspectives, identification of patterns and connections, and elaboration/constructing support.

_____ E. Where appropriate, the teacher involved students in long-term, meaningful-use tasks that included one or more of the following: extended decision making, problem solving, investigation, experimental inquiry, and invention.

_____ F. Assessment and evaluation of student learning were an integral part of all aspects of the lesson; the teacher adjusted the lesson based on ongoing analysis of student behavior as it related to desired outcomes.

_____ G. The overall lesson reflected the following characteristics of effective instruction:

      _____ 1. The instructor established a connection between new and prior learning.

      _____ 2. Questioning techniques reinforced higher-order thinking skills and processes.

      _____ 3. The teacher used a variety of teaching strategies to address the various learning styles and needs present in the classroom.

Comments/Notes:

VI. OUTCOMES OF INSTRUCTION

_____ A. Closure activities allowed students to reflect on lesson objectives and provided teacher with information concerning the effectiveness of the lesson.

_____ B. The teacher used ongoing metacognitive strategies to help students monitor their comprehension and reflect on themselves as learners.

_____ C. Summative assessment ensured that all students mastered the essential learner outcomes identified for the lesson.

_____ D. Where appropriate, the teacher incorporated oral and written communication skills into ongoing assessment practices.

Comments/Notes:

APPENDIX A

Integrating Dimensions of Learning
Into the Formal Teacher Observation Process

The following list of recommendations is designed to complement administrators' and supervisors' use of the observation checklist "Standards for Excellence in Teaching." Both documents are currently in use systemwide in the Prince George's County Public Schools, Maryland. This document will help observers focus on recommendations consistent with the instructional design principles of Dimensions of Learning and the six categories identified in the observation checklist:

- Planning and preparation
- Knowledge
- Classroom management and organization
- Classroom climate
- The process of instruction
- Outcomes of instruction

The suggestions presented here are intended to be examples rather than an all-inclusive list. Commendations and recommendations included in the actual post-observation conference should be consistent with the input and focus areas agreed on by the teacher and observer in their pre-observation conference.

I. PLANNING AND PREPARATION

A. Problem Area: *The teacher fails to prepare a written plan for instruction.*

Possible Recommendations:

- Please consider the use of a written plan for instruction to ensure that your lesson is carefully and consistently organized.
- A written plan for instruction can help you to organize your lesson more effectively.
- Although you may elect to modify it, a written lesson plan can be an invaluable tool to guide your instructional delivery.
- Your written lesson plan should include a clear strategy to focus student attention, objectives stated in behavioral terms, a logically sequenced set of appropriate learning activities, and effective assessment and closure activities.

B. Problem Area: *The lesson lacks a specific task or activity to focus students' attention.*

Possible Recommendations:

- Whenever possible, you should provide some form of warm-up activity or anticipatory set to focus students' learning at the beginning of a lesson.

- In creating an effective warm-up activity, consider what you might have students do to develop positive attitudes and perceptions about the learning climate and the primary learning task they will encounter in the lesson.

- When creating a warm-up or anticipatory set activity, consider the following question: What brief task (up to five minutes) can I use to focus students' attention and prepare them to think critically?

- A warm-up activity should reinforce students' ability to recall and/or apply previously learned declarative and/or procedural knowledge, rather than introducing new learnings.

C. Problem Area: *The lesson objective is not clear, specified, and/or communicated to students.*

Possible Recommendations:

- You should phrase lesson objectives using behavioral verbs that clearly communicate to students what they will know or be able to do as a result of the lesson.

- A learning activity is *not* an objective. An objective is an outcome produced by the instruction you provide. For example, "Read and discuss pages l5–25 in our textbook" is a statement of what you will have students do during the lesson (activity), rather than how they will grow as a result of it (outcome).

- Students should have a clear sense of the outcomes that will result from the lesson. You should explicitly state these outcomes during the initial phase(s) of the lesson, rather than assume that students understand them.

D. Problem Area: *The lesson plan does not contain a clear primary instructional focus or purpose.*

Possible Recommendations:

- An effective lesson should have a clearly understood purpose or focus. Avoid trying to do too much in the time you have with your students.

- Consider focusing each of your lessons on only one of the following so that students have a clear sense of purpose and direction throughout the lesson:
  - Help students master new declarative and/or procedural knowledge.
  - Help students review and reinforce prior declarative and procedural knowledge.
  - Provide clearly specified experiences designed to help students extend and refine essential knowledge through activities involving direct instruction in one or more of the following thinking operations: comparison, classification, induction, deduction, abstraction, elaboration, error analysis, and analysis of perspectives.
  - Introduce and provide time for students to continue their work on a meaningful-use task involving such meta-skills as extended decision making, problem solving, investigation, experimental inquiry, and invention.

—Provide opportunities for students to practice and reflect on productive habits of mind, including self-regulated, critical, and creative thinking.

II. KNOWLEDGE

A. Problem Area: *The teacher does not provide for the learning rates and styles of all students.*

Possible Recommendations:

- Students learn at different rates and in different ways. Please explore ways to vary your instruction to accommodate these differences.

- Some students appeared to be learning the material at the rate at which you presented it. Others appeared to be disengaged or frustrated because they could not keep up. Consider options for accommodating the learning needs of students who require additional time when you are presenting essential declarative and procedural knowledge.

- Much of the current research in cognitive psychology confirms that each student has unique needs, aptitudes, and talents that he or she can demonstrate during the learning process. Please explore ways to address the needs of students who may learn differently than you. For example, many learning style inventories emphasize differences between linear and holistic learners, concrete and abstract learners, and right- and left-hemisphere-dominant learners.

- Consider the use of Contract Activity Packages to respond to individual learning styles and to allow for self-pacing, varied academic levels, independent and self-regulated thinking, and reduced frustration and anxiety.

- Wherever possible, address students' need for multi-sensory learning experiences, including the use of activities that reinforce visual, auditory, and tactile/kinesthetic learning modalities.

B. Problem Area: *The teacher frequently does not use students' names, interact with them, or provide positive verbal and nonverbal feedback.*

Possible Recommendations:

- Using students' names as you interact with them helps to reinforce a positive relationship with each student in the class.

- Please incorporate more cooperative learning strategies and structures into your classroom to enhance your students' interaction with you, their peers, and the material you are presenting.

- Explore TESA (Teacher Expectations and Student Achievement) and GESA (Gender and Ethnic Expectations and Student Achievement) strategies for encouraging positive classroom behavior for all students.

- Incorporate strategies and processes that will allow students in your class to provide positive verbal feedback to their peers. For example, the Bay Area Writing Project uses a "praise, question, and polish" approach to peer response group critiques. First, students praise one or more aspects of the work they have been reviewing; then they pose questions to its author; finally, they propose suggestions for possible revision.

C. Problem Area: *The teacher fails to model techniques and strategies to develop students' critical thinking skills.*

Possible Recommendations:

- Regularly incorporate techniques and strategies designed to reinforce students' critical thinking skills. Review the Maryland State Department of Education bookmark for a list of suggestions.

- Explore strategies that will make instruction in your classroom more student-centered and experience-based. Make certain that your students have an opportunity to enrich their learning through extending/refining activities and meaningful-use tasks.

- Consider incorporating the direct instruction of thinking skills and operations into your classroom practice. For example, if an activity requires students to classify, make certain that students understand the components of that skill and receive a variety of opportunities to model and apply it.

- Integrate strategies to reinforce metacognition and monitor comprehension. Techniques can include think-alouds, KWL's (Know/Want to Know/Learned), reflective journals, think logs, OPVs (DeBono's Opposite Points of View), and others.

D. Problem Area: *The teacher's questions emphasize passive knowledge/recall of information rather than higher-order thinking skills.*

Possible Recommendations:

- Many of your questions emphasized students' passive recall of information they had previously learned. Consider reorienting your questioning process, emphasizing questions that will elicit students' ability to apply, synthesize, analyze, and evaluate knowledge.

- Explore the use of the interpretive question as an essential part of students' reading of a particular text. Such questions should be open-ended, elicit more than a single correct response, and be supportable through textual citations.

- Structure more of your questions to emphasize the Dimensions of Learning extending and refining processes— classification, comparison/contrast, induction, deduction, analysis of perspectives, abstraction, and error analysis.

- Design and use questions that call for thoughtful reflection from your students, particularly at the close of an activity or extended learning experience.

III. CLASSROOM MANAGEMENT

A. Problem Area: *The classroom is poorly organized and fails to support careful management of student behavior.*

Possible Recommendations:

- Consider how you have organized your classroom. Linear rows reinforce the perception of students as isolated elements rather than members of a cohesive whole. Have you considered arranging your students' desks into learning stations of four or five desks? Such an arrangement can make cooperative learning structures much easier to facilitate.

- Explore the use of classroom experiences and activities designed to help students develop a sense of comfort and a positive attitude about learning.

- You might consider helping students develop a sense of order and safety through a clearer delineation of rules, procedures, and classroom policies.

- Make certain that you clearly identify and articulate the specific behaviors expected of students before, during, and after completion of tasks.

- The physical appearance of a classroom can greatly enhance the learning experience for students. Consider the use of bulletin boards, posters, or other displays that can reinforce essential learnings and habits of mind that you wish to emphasize.

B. Problem Area: *There is little variety and an inappropriate quantity of materials of instruction.*

Possible Recommendations:

- Let's explore options for ensuring that every student in your class has his or her own textbook.

- Consider improving students' access to instructional materials through the use of primary source documents, magazines, and related support materials and visuals.

- Explore ways to incorporate nonprint media into your instructional process. Many of your students would benefit from the use of computer software simulations and related forms of educational technology.

C. Problem Area: *A problem with time management is evident.*

Possible Recommendations:

- Pacing is a critical element in an effective lesson. Please plan your lesson so that variety and balance are evident throughout. Don't allow a single activity or issue to inappropriately dominate the instructional experience inappropriately.

- Allow for a variety of learning experiences in the lesson.

- Model for your students a careful attention to time management and closure.

- In cooperative learning groups, appoint a timekeeper who will be responsible for ensuring that students move through the instructional experiences in a timely manner.

- Time spent on task is a critical element for student success. Several of your students engaged in off-task behavior, failing to complete the assignment and engaging in side conversations. Please monitor this behavior more closely to determine their problem(s).

D. Problem Area: *Whole-group, teacher- centered instruction is used throughout the lesson.*

Possible Recommendations:

- Try to get students more actively involved in the instructional process. A majority of classroom time was spent in lecture mode with little opportunity for students to process the material and interact with it.

- Consider the use of a three-minute pause when lecturing. Every ten minutes or so, allow students to break into dyads or triads and respond to the following questions: What are the key ideas, concepts, and issues being presented in the lecture? What areas of the lecture do we have difficulty understanding? What questions about the material would we like answered?

- Vary the pacing of your lesson by integrating large-group, small-group, and individual activities wherever possible.

- Incorporate cooperative learning activities and structures to allow students a more active role in the instructional process. Consider such processes as think-pair-shares, student team learning, and jigsaw activities, in which students become experts on a key topic or skill and teach one another.

- Explore the use of student conferences as a vehicle for individualizing the instructional process and for encouraging reflective practice.

- Vary the pacing of your classroom by interjecting student-centered learning experiences, including techniques like student calling, student-generated goals and activities, and the use of students' interests and knowledge as a basis for shaping and defining lesson content.

IV. CLASSROOM CLIMATE

A. Problem Area: *The teacher fails to incorporate Dimension 1 techniques to create a positive and productive classroom climate.*

Possible Recommendations:

- Be careful to monitor your attitudes toward certain students so that you do not communicate unconscious negative expectations about them.

- Work with students to help them use strategies and techniques for gaining acceptance by their peers, particularly as you monitor cooperative learning activities.

- Wherever possible, you might consider the use of activities that involve the appropriate use of physical movement.

- Many students expressed a feeling that they could not understand or be successful at the activities you assigned. Work with them on bracketing—that is, minimizing the effect of distracting or disturbing thoughts so that they can attend to instructional tasks.

- Please work on providing positive feedback to all students to reinforce their belief that they have the ability and resources to succeed in your classroom.

- Identify and articulate the specific behaviors you expect of students during and after successful completion of tasks.

- Where appropriate, break complex tasks into small steps or parts.

B. Problem Area: *The classroom environment does not invite learning and does not help students develop a sense of comfort and order.*

Possible Recommendations:

- You were inconsistent in your expectations of different students in your classroom. Make sure that every student is invited to become an active part of the learning process.

- Use interactive assessment techniques to monitor student progress. For example, you can use Madeline Hunter's "thumbs up/thumbs down" technique to sample students' reaction to a learning task or to assess which students feel they understand or don't understand a key concept or skill.

- Make use of various cooperative learning strategies and structures to encourage students to actively construct meaning. For example, you might consider using the "numbered heads together" technique to encourage student to process a key idea or principle.

- You might consider getting students more involved in helping to establish the culture and climate of your classroom. For example, you might have students develop personal standards for comfort and order and, where appropriate, integrate them into classroom rules and procedures.

C. Problem Area: *The teacher does not reflect the attitude that all students can learn.*

Possible Recommendations:

- You seemed to call on relatively few students during the lesson, allowing two or three to dominate. Consider ways to make your classroom more equitable. Random calling during questioning, for example, or allowing those students answering a question to determine who responds next can help you break such a pattern.

- Several of your students remained out of the discussion loop throughout the lesson. Consider ways you might have brought them into the conversation.

- Explore ways to draw on students' individual strengths in classroom activities. For example, in forming groups, consider balancing a highly extroverted student who has a skills deficiency with a more introverted student who is highly able in that area.

- A few students appeared to dominate the classroom while many students remained generally uninvolved. Explore ways to ensure that all students are an active part of the instructional process.

- Have you noticed that you tend to call on (male students/female students) more often than you call on (male students/female students)? Is there a pattern here, or was this lesson an exception? Such a pattern seemed to be present in your lesson today.

- In this lesson, you consistently emphasized atomistic, micro-level skills and information rather than larger connecting themes, principles, concepts, and meta-skills. Consider the use of activities and strategies designed to help students master higher-order declarative and procedural knowledge, rather than exclusively focusing on basic knowledge/recall activities.

D. Problem Area: *There is little evidence of displays that reflect the subject area and reinforce key learnings.*

Possible Recommendations:

- Consider creating displays in your classroom that reflect key elements of what students are studying.

- A powerful meaningful-use task might be to have students develop two- and three-dimensional displays that reflect key concepts, principles, generalizations, and processes studied during one or more units. Your classroom can become a gallery of student work reflecting how students have constructed meaning in response to your course content.

- Explore ways for students to work together to decorate your room so that it reflects your immediate and long-range instructional priorities.

- Student-designed bulletin boards can be powerful vehicles for reflecting current and future instructional priorities and directions.

E. Problem Area: *The classroom is not clean and orderly.*

Possible Recommendations:

- The design, organization, and overall condition of your classroom play a powerful role in determining classroom climate and culture. Please explore ways to improve in these areas, particularly by making your classroom a clean and orderly place for student learning.

- You might designate classroom monitors to help manage materials and evaluate the condition of the environment at the conclusion of specific learning activities.

- Discuss with your students the importance of maintaining a clean and orderly environment in the classroom. Use these sessions as a way to encourage active problem solving and decision making.

- If a particular class seems especially hard on classroom order and cleanliness, consider a town meeting simulation that will allow students to explore ways to help you and one another maintain a more orderly learning environment.

V. THE PROCESS OF INSTRUCTION

A. Problem Area: *Introductory and developmental activities are not organized to ensure student mastery of essential learner outcomes.*

Possible Recommendations:

- The introductory and developmental activities presented in your lesson were not clearly aligned with and supportive of the objectives you identified for the class.

- Students appeared to have trouble relating the introductory activities to the objectives you presented. You might wish to use a more interactive approach to monitor student comprehension, to ensure that all students are following the instructional process. Can all students clearly identify the purpose of what they are doing as it relates to your identified outcome statements?

- Please work on scaffolding and bridging for students the transitions between and among instructional activities. Each section of your lesson should have a clear and expressed relationship between your identified objectives and the specific learning activities and tasks assigned to students.

- Consider integrating ongoing formative assessment into all facets of the lesson to ensure that students are constructing meaning for themselves and are able to identify the purpose(s) of what they are doing.

- Make an attempt to tie your individual lesson to the overall unit in which it is presented. Several of your students expressed some confusion about the way in which your introductory and developmental activities were related to what they had been working on within the last week(s).

B. Problem Area: *Students appear to have difficulty constructing meaning, organizing information, and storing it in long-term memory.*

Possible Recommendations:

- Your lesson concentrated heavily on students learning a large body of declarative knowledge (i.e., facts, concepts, generalizations, principles). You might wish to reduce the coverage of so much information in favor of a focused study of essential declarative knowledge organized in a more coherent fashion. In particular, you might help students understand the value and relevance of the content and activities presented in the lesson, especially how those elements relate to their own lives and experiences.

- Students need help identifying general topics and specifics in your lesson. Please be more specific about the *essential* facts, concepts, generalizations, and principles you wish to emphasize in the lesson. In addition, please be very explicit about the *exact* declarative knowledge students should store in long-term memory.

- Please explore a more expanded approach to helping students construct meaning in relationship to essential declarative knowledge. You might wish to include such strategies as the three-minute pause, use of sensory experiences, KWL (Know/Want to Know/Learned) activities, concept attainment and inquiry-based instruction, reciprocal teaching, and Before/During/After strategies.

- Students appeared to have difficulty organizing the declarative knowledge you presented. Consider an expanded use of physical and pictographic representations, particularly graphic organizers and flow charts.

- Consider the use of memory recall devices to help students learn to store declarative knowledge in long-term memory. There is enormous benefit to having students master and use such techniques as the rhyming pegword system, number/picture system, familiar place system, and link strategies.

C. Problem Area: *Students appear to have difficulty learning essential skills, processes, and procedures.*

Possible Recommendations:

- Your lesson should clearly identify for students the essential or core procedural knowledge they will need to learn and apply during the period.

- Students would benefit from a more careful modeling of the key skills and processes you wish them to learn and apply during the lesson. Techniques to enhance their mastery of this procedural knowledge can include think-alouds, presenting students with a written set of steps, having students create flow charts, and having students mentally rehearse the steps involved in a skill or process.

- Practice or shaping of skills is a vital part of skills mastery. Please work on helping students to shape procedural knowledge by demonstrating and providing practice in the important variations of the skill or process; demonstrating common errors or pitfalls in the use of a skill or process; and having students use essential skills or processes in different situations, with appropriate scaffolding to ensure effective transfer.

- Work with students to help them internalize procedural knowledge more effectively. For example, you might have them set up a practice schedule, chart their accuracy when practicing new skills or processes, and chart their speed when learning a new skill or process.

D. Problem Area: *Instruction fails to emphasize the ability of students to extend and refine their use of essential knowledge.*

Possible Recommendations:

- Many of your students would benefit from coaching designed to help them understand and master the use of such essential thinking processes as comparison, classification, analysis of perspectives, and other types of cognitive processes.

- Please work with your students to identify and apply the elements or steps in such critical thinking processes as induction, deduction, and error analysis.

- Ask students more extending and refining questions before, during, and after an important learning experience; make certain that these questions relate directly to the essential thinking process(es) students must use during the lesson.

- During this lesson, your students would have benefited from more direct instruction in the use of the following thinking process(es):
  - *Comparison*: identifying similarities and differences
  - *Classification*: categorizing elements according to clearly specified characteristics
  - *Induction*: investigating information and drawing inferences and conclusions based on that information
  - *Deduction*: developing arguments and specific statements from generalizations and principles, including the use of syllogistic reasoning
  - *Analyzing errors*, including the identification and evaluation of fallacies in reasoning or logic
  - *Constructing support*: elaborating on or backing up generalizations and conclusions, including the development of persuasive arguments
  - *Abstracting*: identifying general patterns and connections
  - *Analyzing perspectives*: identifying and evaluating points of view and perspectives associated with a controversial issue or topic, including biases and values implicit in a reading selection or oral presentation

- You can help students extend and refine higher-order thinking processes by using one or more of the following techniques:
  - Directly introducing an essential thinking process to students
  - Presenting students with a written set of steps associated with the process
  - Providing students with ways of graphically representing the process
  - Presenting students with teacher-constructed tasks related to the process
  - Presenting students with student-structured activities related to the process
  - Presenting students with expanded process-based activities

E. Problem Area: *The instructor fails to integrate meaningful-use tasks into his or her long-range unit planning.*

Possible Recommendations:

- Students would benefit from a greater instructional focus on meaningful-use tasks— that is, long-term, student-directed, experiential learning, and reality-based activities that allow students to demonstrate alternative approaches to dealing with meta-skills such as the following:
  - *Decision making*, including the use of a coherent model of decision making and its application to real-world decisions and situations

- *Investigation*, including extensive use of historical, definitional, and projective investigations centered around individual inquiry
- *Problem solving*, including the modeling of steps in the problem-solving process and experience with unstructured problem tasks
- *Experimental inquiry*, including both teacher-structured and student-structured experiments
- *Invention*, including formative and summative assessment tasks that involve the creation of new products or works

- Encourage students to understand the purpose and usefulness of the tasks in which they are engaged by helping them experience real-world applications and connections.

- The culmination of a meaningful-use task should be a student-directed product and/or process, as well as some form of oral defense or presentation.

F. Problem Area: *The instructor fails to adjust the lesson in response to ongoing analysis of student behavior relative to designated outcomes.*

Possible Recommendations:

- Evaluation of your lesson seems to concentrate almost exclusively on the desired end product. Please incorporate processes to provide yourself with input throughout the lesson concerning how students are mastering identified objectives.

- Please monitor student progress from the beginning to the end of the lesson. Explore an expanded use of formative assessment strategies in your lesson.

- Work on integrating metacognitive strategies into your assessment process so that students can express and monitor their own comprehension and assess themselves as learners. Such strategies might include think-alouds, reflective journals and think logs, process reflection, and think-pair-shares, among others.

- Consider incorporating oral activities into your assessment repertoire.

- You might consider using the summative evaluation component of your lesson as a closure activity involving all members of the class in some form of cooperative learning structure. Dyads or triads, for example, might identify what they consider to be the most important knowledge they gained during the lesson. You might also have groups evaluate the extent to which stated objectives were achieved.

G. Problem Area: *The overall lesson fails to reflect one or more of the characteristics of effective instruction.*

Possible Recommendations:

- Please work with students to help them establish connections between new and prior learning. Such scaffolding is a critical part of effective instruction.

- Explore ways to expand your use of different types of questions. Many of the questions you posed during the lesson asked students simply to recall information. You might consider a greater use of interpretive, analytical, and evaluative questions to expand students' learning experiences during the lesson.

- Wherever possible, use a variety of teaching strategies to address the diverse learning styles and needs present in your classroom. Try to vary instruction, for example, to accommodate the needs of the student who learns through a dominant learning channel (e.g., auditory, visual, tactile/kinesthetic). Also, please consider the needs of the concrete learner who requires an explicit and specific step-by-step approach to instruction, versus the more abstract, nonlinear student who is capable of immediate intuitive leaps. Build in opportunities for students to expand and elaborate upon what they have learned through creative and artistic expressions, products, and processes.

VI. OUTCOMES OF INSTRUCTION

A. Problem Area: *The lesson lacked some form of closure.*

Possible Recommendations:

- Consider the way you bring your lesson to a close. Wherever possible, use closure activities that allow students to reflect on lesson objectives and that provide you with information about the effectiveness of the lesson.

- Design closure activities to foster a sense of completion among students in your class. Such activities may be an essential part of the assessment process or they can function as a stand-alone process.

- As part of an effective closure activity, you might ask students to explore with you one or more of the following questions:
  - What did we do during this class session that was particularly important or relevant to you?
  - How far will we go tomorrow? For our next lesson, think about . . .
  - In your opinion, what are the most significant or interesting parts of the lesson?
  - How does this lesson relate to you and the world you inhabit?
  - If you were to design a test for the class on today's lesson, what questions or activities would you include?

B. Problem Area: *Students receive little support in monitoring their own comprehension and reflecting on themselves as learners.*

Possible Recommendations:

- Please integrate opportunities for metacognitive reflection throughout your lesson. Without the chance to monitor their own comprehension, students may find it difficult to identify what they are accomplishing and what help they need to learn identified objectives.

- Effective formative assessment should include options for metacognitive reflection. Such options might include
  - Think logs
  - Reflective journals
  - Process observations and reflections
  - KWL's
  - Free writing
  - Think-alouds
  - Cooperative, learning-based group discussion and reflection about key elements of the lesson

- Use metacognitive processes to help students reflect on and reinforce their development of productive mental habits—that is, self-regulated, critical, and creative thinking.

- Provide opportunities for students to internalize and demonstrate their proficiency in productive mental habits by
  - Identifying mental habits essential to success within a subject or discipline.
  - Having students identify situations in which specific mental habits would be useful.
  - Having students develop strategies and techniques to help them use these mental habits.
  - Having students identify and pursue long-term goals related to these mental habits.
  - Appointing process observers to identify examples of specific mental habits that occur during classroom activities.

- Work with your students to help them become more self-regulated in their thinking by helping them to
  - Be aware of their own thinking.
  - Plan.
  - Be aware of necessary resources.
  - Be sensitive and responsive to feedback.
  - Evaluate the effectiveness of their own actions.

- Work with your students to help them become more effective critical thinkers by helping them to
  - Be accurate and seek accuracy.
  - Be clear and seek clarity.
  - Be open-minded.
  - Restrain impulsivity.
  - Take a position when the situation warrants it.

- Work with your students to demonstrate creative thinking by helping them to
  - Engage intensely in tasks even when answers or solutions are not immediately apparent.
  - Push the limits of their own knowledge and abilities.
  - Generate, trust, and maintain their own standards of evaluation.
  - Generate new ways of viewing a situation outside the boundaries of standard conventions.

D. Problem area: *Summative assessment does not ensure that all students mastered the essential learner outcomes identified for the lesson.*

Possible Recommendations:

- Your lesson contained no method, instrument, or process to determine how well all of your students did in achieving the learning the objectives identified for the lesson.

- Build into every lesson some method for determining how well each of your students performed in relation to identified learner outcomes. Such summative evaluation can include oral and written processes as well as metacognitive reflection at the individual, small-group, and full-group level.

- Wherever possible, use performance-based tasks as a vehicle for determining how students internalized, constructed meaning around, and can apply the essential knowledge taught and/or reinforced during the lesson.

- Summative evaluation should also consider how students are able to connect new learning to prior knowledge acquired during the unit. Use your evaluation process as a method to reinforce and establish connections between and among various parts of your unit and course.

E. Problem Area: *Oral and written communication skills are not incorporated into ongoing assessment practices.*

Possible Recommendations

- Summative evaluation activities are wonderful opportunities to reinforce for students the value of oral and written communication.

- Consider a greater use of writing activities as a basis for monitoring and evaluating student progress in relationship to your lesson, unit, and course outcomes.

- Periodically use both formative and summative evaluation activities as an opportunity to reinforce students' ability to express themselves in both formal and informal oral communication settings and processes.

References and Resources

ASCD. (1987/1989). *The Teaching Strategies Library* (two four-part videotape programs with Trainer's Manuals). Alexandria, Va.: ASCD.

ASCD. (1988). *The Video Library of Teaching Episodes* (videotape program). Alexandria, Va.: ASCD.

ASCD. (1989a). *Another Set of Eyes: Conferencing Skills* (three-tape videotape program with trainer's manual). Alexandria, Va.: ASCD.

ASCD. (1989b). *Another Set of Eyes: Techniques for Classroom Observation* (two-tape videotape program with trainer's manual). Alexandria, Va.: ASCD.

ASCD. (1989c). *Opening Doors: An Introduction to Peer Coaching* (two-tape videotape program with Facilitator's Manual). Alexandria, Va.: ASCD.

ASCD. (1992a). *Dimensions of Learning Videotape Package* (six videotapes). Alexandria, Va.: ASCD.

ASCD. (1992b). *Involving Parents in Education* (30-minute videotape program with facilitator's guide). Alexandria, Va.: ASCD.

ASCD. (1992c). *Outcome-Based Education* (four-tape videotape program with Facilitator's Guide). Alexandria, Va.: ASCD.

ASCD. (1992d). *Redesigning Assessment* (three-tape videotape program with a facilitator's guide for each tape). Alexandria, Va.: ASCD.

ASCD. (1993a). *Changing Schools Through Shared Decision Making* (two-tape videotape program with Facilitator's Guide). Alexandria, Va.: ASCD.

ASCD. (1993b). *Integrating the Curriculum* (two-tape videotape program with Facilitator's Guide). Alexandria, Va.: ASCD.

ASCD. (1993c). *Schools of Quality* (videotape with Facilitator's Guide). Alexandria, Va.: ASCD.

ASCD. (1995). *Action Research: Inquiry, Reflection, and Decision Making* (four-tape videotape program with Facilitator's Guide). Alexandria, Va.: ASCD.

Bostingl, J.J. (1992). *Schools of Quality: An Introduction to Total Quality Management in Education.* Alexandria, Va.: ASCD.

Calhoun, E.F. (1994). *How to Use Action Research in the Self-Renewing School.* Alexandria, Va.: ASCD.

Calhoun, E.F., and C.G. Glickman. (1993). "Issues and Dilemmas of Action Research in the League of Professional Schools." Paper presented at the annual meeting of the American Educational Research Association, Atlanta.

Cogan, M. (1973). *Clinical Supervision.* Boston: Houghton Mifflin.

Costa, A.L., and R.J. Garmston. (1994). *Cognitive Coaching: A Foundation for Renaissance Schools.* Norwood, Mass.: Christopher-Gordon.

Covey, S.R. (1990). *The 7 Habits of Highly Effective People.* New York: Simon and Schuster.

Covey, S.R. (1992). *Principle-Centered Leadership.* New York: Fireside Press.

English, F.W. (1992). *Guidebooks to Effective Educational Leadership, Vol.2: Deciding What to Teach and Test—Developing, Aligning, and Auditing the Curriculum.* Newbury Park, Calif.: Corwin Press.

Futrell, M.H., P.C. Schlecty, J. Hixson, A. Lieberman, L. Miller, A.L. Costa, S.D. Caldwell, S.S. Ellis, and M. Hunter. (Winter 1991). "Nine Perspectives on the Future of Staff Development." *Journal of Staff Development* 12, 1: 2–9.

Gardner, H. (1983). *Frames of Mind: The Theory of Multiple Intelligences*. New York: Basic Books.

Glatthorn, A.A. (1987a). *Curriculum Leadership*. New York: Harper-Collins.

Glatthorn, A.A. (1987b). *Curriculum Renewal*. Alexandria, Va.: ASCD.

Glattorn, A.A. (1994). *Developing a Quality Curriculum*. Alexandria, Va.: ASCD.

Glickman, C.D. (1990). *Supervision of Instruction: A Developmental Approach*. Boston: Allyn and Bacon.

Goldhammer, R. (1969). *Clinical Supervision: Special Method for the Supervision of Teachers*. New York: Holt, Rinehart, and Winston.

Goswami, D., and P.R. Stillman, eds. (1987). *Reclaiming the Classroom: Teacher Research as an Agency for Change*. Portsmouth, N.H.: Boynton/Cook Publishers.

Herman, J.L., P.R. Aschbacher, and L. Winters. (1992). *A Practical Guide to Alternative Assessment*. Alexandria, Va.: ASCD.

Hopkins, D. (1992). *A Teacher's Guide to Classroom Research*. 2nd ed. Philadelphia: Open University Press.

Hord, S.M., W.L. Rutherford, L. Huling-Austin, and G.E. Hall. (1987). *Taking Charge of Change*. Alexandria, Va.: ASCD.

Hunter, M. (1982). *Mastery Teaching*. El Segundo, Calif.: TIP Publications.

Joyce, B., J. Wolf, and E. Calhoun. (1993). *The Self-Renewing School*. Alexandria, Va.: ASCD.

Kinlaw, D.C. (1992). *Continuous Improvement and Measurement for Total Quality: A Team-Based Approach*. San Diego: Pfeiffer Company.

Kline, P. and B. Saunders. (1993). *Ten Steps to a Learning Organization*. Arlington, Va.: Great Ocean Publishers.

Lieberman, A., ed. (1988). *Building a Professional Culture in Schools*. New York: Teachers College Press.

Marburger, C.L. (1989). *One School at a Time: School Based Management—A Process for Change*. Columbia, Md.: The National Committee for Citizens in Education.

Marzano, R.J. (1992). *A Different Kind of Classroom: Teaching with Dimensions of Learning*. Alexandria, Va.: ASCD..

Marzano, R.J., D.J. Pickering, D.E. Arredondo, G.J. Blackburn, R.S. Brandt, and C.A. Moffett. (1992a). *Dimensions of Learning Teacher's Manual*. Alexandria, Va.: ASCD.

Marzano, R.J., D.J. Pickering, D.E. Arredondo, G.J. Blackburn, R.S. Brandt, and C.A. Moffett. (1992b). *Implementing Dimensions of Learning*. Alexandria, Va: ASCD.

Marzano, R.J., D.J. Pickering, and J. McTighe. (1993). *Assessing Student Outcomes: Performance Assessment Using the Dimensions of Learning Model*. Alexandria, Va: ASCD.

Oakes, J. (1985). *Keeping Track: How Schools Structure Inequality*. New Haven: Yale University Press.

Oja, S.N., and L. Smulyan. (1989.) *Collaborative Action Research: A Developmental Approach*. New York: The Falmer Press.

Resnick, L.B., and L.E. Klopfer, eds. (1989). *Toward the Thinking Curriculum: Current Cognitive Research. 1989 ASCD Yearbook*. Alexandria, Va.: ASCD.

Schein, E.H. (1992). *Organizational Culture and Leadership*. 2nd ed. New York: The Jossey-Bass Management Series.

Schön, D.A. (1982). *The Reflective Practitioner: How Professionals Think in Action*. New York: Basic Books.

Senge, P.M. (1990). *The Fifth Discipline: The Art and Practice of the Learning Organization*. New York: Doubleday, Currency.

Sikes, W., A.B. Drexler, and J. Gant. (1989). *The Emerging Practice of Organization Development.* Alexandria, Va.: National Training Labs Institute for Applied Behavioral Science.

Sizer, T.R. (1992). *Horaces' School: Redesigning the American High School.* Boston: Houghton Mifflin.

Wiggins, G. (1991). "Teaching to the (Authentic) Test." In *Developing Minds: A Resource Book for Teaching Thinking,* Vol. 1, revised ed. Alexandria, Va.: ASCD.

About the Author

John L. Brown is Supervisor of Curriculum and Program Development for the Prince George's County Public Schools in Maryland. In that capacity, he is responsible for managing curriculum development, new and emerging programs, and staff development in the following areas: Dimensions of Learning, strategies for improving thinking, learning styles, performance-based instruction and assessment, and strategic planning. Brown has consulted with schools throughout the United States on the implementation of Dimensions of Learning and is also an Adjunct Professor in Curriculum Theory and Development at Johns Hopkins University in Baltimore, Maryland, and at Trinity College in Washington, D.C. He is completing his Ph.D. in education at George Mason University, Fairfax, Virginia. He can be reached at (301) 808-8261.

About ASCD

Founded in 1943, the Association for Supervision and Curriculum Development is a nonpartisan, nonprofit education association, with international headquarters in Alexandria, Virginia. ASCD's mission statement: *ASCD, a diverse, international community of educators, forging covenants in teaching and learning for the success of all learners.*

Membership in ASCD includes a subscription to the award-winning journal *Educational Leadership*; two newsletters, *Education Update* and *Curriculum Update*; and other products and services. ASCD sponsors affiliate organizations in many states and international locations; participates in collaborations and networks; holds conferences, institutes, and training programs; produces publications in a variety of media; sponsors recognition and awards programs; and provides research information on education issues.

ASCD provides many services to educators—prekindergarten through grade 12—as well as others in the education community, including parents, school board members, administrators, and university professors and students. For further information about ASCD, call (703) 549-9110 or fax (703) 299-8631. Internet access: gopher.ascd.org. Or write to ASCD, Information Services, 1250 N. Pitt St., Alexandria, VA 22314.

1995–96 ASCD Executive Council

President: Charles E. Patterson, Superintendent, Killeen Independent School District, Killeen, Texas

President-Elect: Frances Faircloth Jones, Executive Director, Piedmont Triad Horizons Educational Consortium, University of North Carolina, Greensboro, North Carolina

Immediate Past President: Arthur Steller, Deputy Superintendent, Boston Public Schools, Boston, Massachusetts

Janice Adkisson, Staff Development/Early Childhood Supervisor, Arlington County Public Schools, Arlington, Virginia

M. Kay Awalt, Principal, Moore Elementary School, Franklin, Tennessee

Brenda Benson-Burrell, Associate Professor, College of Education, Wayne State University, Detroit, Michigan

Marge Chow, Superintendent, Richland Public Schools, Richland, Washington

Douglas Gruber, Superintendent of Program Services, Waterloo Region RCSS Board, Kitchner, Ontario, Canada

Edward Hall, Assistant Superintendent for Instruction, Curriculum, and Staff Development, Talladega County Board of Education, Talladega, Alabama

Joanna Choi Kalbus, University Lecturer, University of California-Riverside, California

Margret Montgomery, President, Professional Research Institute, Austin, Texas

David Rainey, Director, Arkansas Math/Science School, Hot Springs, Arkansas

Charles Schwahn, Leadership, Management, and Organization Development Consultant, Custer, South Dakota

Judy Stevens, Executive Director of Elementary Education, Spring Branch Independent School District, Houston, Texas

Sherrelle J. Walker, Assistant Superintendent, Federal Way School District, Federal Way, Washington

Isa Kaftal Zimmerman, Superintendent of Schools, Acton Public Schools and Acton-Boxborough Regional Schools, Acton, Massachusetts